value the
architecture,
weathering and use
and allow for
of peace or insight.
supports slowness in
in the important
and construction,
that human habitation
needs time.

KT-423-290

This is a gently serious architecture that connects geometry and order to ideas of landscape and nature, that stimulates our senses and that positively fuses tradition with invention and the new.

Invigorated by foreign influences, cool construction is less about regionalism and more about the application of form to indigenous climate, topography and patterns of use.

These practitioners
longevity of
respect the effects of
upon buildings,
special moments
Their attitude
architecture, slowness
processes of design
and an understanding
of the environment

Avoiding strange or jarringly foreign materials, these architects re-present building processes to aid human understanding. The visual is paramount and unashamed. Historical appreciation and spatial rigour give the work its timeless character.

Cool construction
tactile way.
body to roam
An architecture of
is content to reveal
of material –
clothing – in both
horizontal planes.
planes physically
and stairs,
through the
light and shade, so
of architecture is

engages us in a
It encourages the
and explore.
slow beauty
the sedimentation
like layers of
the vertical and
It connects those
with ramps
and visually
orchestration of
that the experience
kinetic and sensual.

Neither tied to the past nor shockingly new, neither decorative nor dogmatic, these works allow beauty to emerge from the natural or atmospheric conditions of site, from the interconnection of programme, from rational composition and from construction itself.

Cool
Construction

Raymund Ryan

Cool
Construction

With 284 illustrations, 124 in colour

Thames & Hudson

Contents

4.11

4.12

4.13

4.14

4.21

4.22

4.23

Cool Construction:
An Architecture of Slow Beauty

There is a new spirit emerging in architecture, an ethic and pleasure in construction that simultaneously values progress and the eternal. In cool construction, the entirety of a building is greater than the sum of its parts. The role or position of the human being is privileged. This is a gently serious architecture that connects geometry and order to ideas of landscape and nature, that fully engages our senses and that positively fuses tradition or the timeless with invention and the new.

At the centre of Berlin, the nineteenth-century Neues Museum (p. 42) is being reconfigured for the modern era by British architect David Chipperfield, who envisages the museum and its symbolic position on the Museuminsel (Museum Island) as a family of interconnected pavilions or fragments, each with its own character. The result promises to be a volumetric network in which new and old, the abstract and the figurative merge to form an integrated urban assemblage that shows many carefully arranged layers of building history. Chipperfield has the good sense to allow context and content – fundamental to the purpose of the museum – to maintain a certain visible dignity. His work gains by being contingent upon the existing fabric.

Across the world in Kyoto, a renowned Japanese restaurant Murasakino Wakuden (p. 56) is located in a new concrete tower with horizontal chestnut siding and limited fenestration. It is rather enigmatic and surprisingly abstract for an established gourmet business. Waro Kishi has placed one small window at ground level to display delicacies to passers-by and has then opened up a vertical crevicelike courtyard that leads to an entry hall where guests are received and lunch boxes picked up. Meals are served at a bar upstairs, in a hushed shady space with tall red timber chairs, and are prepared in a private kitchen on the floor above. Light filters in through floor-to-ceiling windows screened by louvres. Directly across the street is the ancient Daitoku-ji temple complex.

Back in Europe, in the rainy countryside of northern Portugal, Eduardo Souto de Moura has spent ten years reassembling what was the derelict monastery of Santa Maria do Bouro (p. 80). He has inserted new structure, new materials and new services to make the historic shell habitable as an elegant modern hotel (in Portuguese, a *pousada*). Occasionally the architect's interventions are clearly visible and inviting to be touched; but they can also be almost imperceptible. Souto de Moura's work has this paradoxical intent: although he is resolute about practical issues of construction, he likes to play with human perception. The apparent simplicity of his forms belies a visual intelligence informed by recent minimalist and conceptual art.

4.00 Pousada Santa Maria
do Bouro, Eduardo Souto
de Moura [this page]
Rua do Teatro Apartments,
Eduardo Souto de Moura
[opposite]

On a third continent, in La Jolla, California, Tod Williams and Billie Tsien have built a new multi-part building that also addresses issues of human use and cognition. The Neurosciences Institute (NSI, p. 104) unfolds as a series of interrelated forms around a sun-filled plaza. It is a complex topographic settlement. As with most projects by the New York–based architects, the idea of the architectural promenade, proposed by Le Corbusier in the 1920s, is developed at various scales and across many surfaces throughout the entire volume and site. Williams and Tsien's design entices movement and reveals itself to the mobile observer at different moments: moments as places of specific architectural quality and moments as conscious episodes in time.

The Neues Museum, the traditional restaurant, the pousada and the research institute are exemplary models of a cool manipulation of construction techniques and a renewed appreciation of the inherent beauty of material. This is an architecture that becomes meaningful slowly, through use.

Place

These architects, whose work is evolving toward a more humane, integrated environment, are based in different countries and ecologies but share certain essential concerns. It may be that Kishi's meticulously crafted projects are more feasible in Japan, where practical and aesthetic concerns support the degree of care he devotes to each work. Kishi might quickly reply, however, that he is equally engaged with the trajectory of Eurocentric architectural culture, that Westerners need not be sycophantic toward the East. Today, the local need be neither provincial nor anachronistic. In this era of advanced capitalism and instantaneous communication networks, we are all world citizens.

The arrival of postmodernism in architectural debate in the 1970s marked a shift away from strict functionalism, from the one-to-one relationship, instigated by the Bauhaus between form and programme, between structure and space. Cognisant of the destruction of the fabric of traditional cities by modernization, persuaded by growing academic interest in semiotics and linguistics, and conscious of the lack of any single theory or explanation of how the world might be, postmodernism brought everything together in historically eclectic ways. Above all, it emphasized the façade and the visual to the extent that – for all its ambitions toward legibility – it is seldom clear of what these skin-deep buildings actually consist. Today, with globalization, postmodern projects look uncannily alike.

Everywhere is becoming increasingly similar. In the 1960s, this homogenization of the world was discussed by the French philosopher Paul Ricoeur in his essay 'Universal Civilization and National Culture'.[1] Ricoeur's unease with the disappearance of local character was reiterated in the 1980s by the architectural historian Kenneth Frampton, who coined the phrase 'critical regionalism' to categorize an architecture providing 'resistance' to the placelessness of so many postwar institutions and precincts.[2] Cool construction is less about regionalism, and the political connotations that

go with it, and more about the application of form to indigenous climate, topography and patterns of use.

Invigorated by foreign influences, the work of Souto de Moura is entwined with a profound understanding of constructional capabilities in modern Portugal. Williams and Tsien could only have designed the comparatively low-budget Freeman Silverman House (p. 110) near Phoenix after a close analysis of weather, the movement of the sun and water levels on the site.

Proof of their attention to place, the architects featured here often set limits or boundaries to their projects, which act as internalizing enclosures and as framing devices to an exterior fluid world (Chipperfield has acknowledged his appropriation of such tactics from Japan). Furthermore, the tectonics of building – the manner in which components of structure and skin are assembled and expressed – is a primary concern. Avoiding strange or jarringly foreign materials, these architects re-present building processes to aid human understanding. With a sensuous interpretation of such modernist masters as Le Corbusier and Ludwig Mies van der Rohe, they have also absorbed a postmodern appreciation of history and local colour. It is curiously this renewed appreciation, together with spatial rigour, that give the work its timeless character.

Time

As the speed and efficiency of communications increase, time seems to be less and less real. Jet travel, satellites and the Internet have radically altered the nature of connections between people. Today there is a dizzying rush, a vertigo almost, about life, work schedules and data or information transferral. Several international architects have embraced this technocratic speed to interesting effect. Others take a different, possibly more critical, view that values the longevity of architecture, respects the effects of weathering and use upon buildings, and allows for special moments of peace or insight. This attitude supports slowness in architecture, slowness in the important processes of design and construction, and an understanding that human habitation of the environment needs time.

Cool construction engages the human spirit in a tactile way. It encourages the body to roam and explore, as in Chipperfield's Neues Museum proposal. An architecture of slow beauty is content to reveal the sedimentation of material – like layers of clothing – in both the vertical and horizontal planes. It connects those planes physically with ramps and stairs, and visually through the orchestration of light and shade, so that the experience of architecture is kinetic and sensual. Architecture achieves its full meaning or potential through a physical discovery of space and surface in time, as shown in such projects as Waro Kishi's Memorial Hall at Yamaguchi University (p. 60) and Tod Williams and Billie Tsien's Neurosciences Institute. It represents a re-evaluation of the importance – first discussed in the early-twentieth century by philosopher Henri Bergson – of *la durée*, of duration.

Appreciation of time brings cool construction alive. In Kishi's work, time is evident in the conscious reworking of traditions (classic and vernacular) and in the ability, over a period of time, to experience subtleties of illumination within and about his architecture. In Japan, tradition is not index-linked to age. The value of time is associated with a certain spirit of place and the ritual of making (at the shrine at Ise, not far from Kyoto, the famous timber structure is replicated on an adjacent site every twenty years). The buildings of these architects are never faux-historic. While one may be reminded of Martin Heidegger's seminal text *Bauen Wohnen Denken*,[3] with its profound concern for dwelling, these projects also have an inherent sense of movement. Souto de Moura, for instance, reduces the floors, walls and ceilings of his Courtyard Housing (p. 90) at Matosinhos to smooth planes that encourage, through shadow and illumination, a progression toward natural light.

For these architects, space is more important than any static object. By unfolding the Neurosciences Institute into several parts, sections of the programme are identified but, more importantly, a communal space for the institution is created. Backing up toward a roadway, the NSI harnesses topography and pedestrian routes so that it becomes a great clock tracking movement and light. Williams and Tsien are currently constructing the Museum of American Folk Art (p. 118) with a similarly intense procession, albeit in a vertical sequence sandwiched between tall neighbours in midtown Manhattan. Neither it nor the NSI can be understood from any single vantage point or photograph – they both have to be moved through to be fully comprehended. In these small daily journeys, in what the Polish poet Zbigniew Herbert called the 'holy ritual of everydayness',[4] the beauty of architecture slowly reveals itself to touch and sight.

Beauty

Since earliest recorded times, artists and philosophers, from Plato and Aristotle through Hegel to the present, have debated the definition and value of beauty. Until comparatively recently, art aspired to create beautiful objects – temples, statues, paintings, ceremonial pieces – in which proportion and surface treatments were perfected to often pre-established types. Aesthetics and ethics were closely related. Truth was regularly coupled with beauty. In the twentieth century, the foppish adage of 'art for art's sake' withered before the raw reality of daily life. Beauty seemed of minor significance to the planners of functionalist objects and workers' utopias. What use was beauty to problems of sanitation and mass production? However, dissatisfaction with a characterless and placeless environment now allows for a reassessment of beauty's role. Architecture can again be more than mere practicality.

Today's architecture is characterized by its balance of essential concerns: construction, landscape, time, the beautiful. Neither tied to the past nor shockingly new, neither decorative nor dogmatic, the work of the four practices allows beauty to emerge from the natural or atmospheric conditions

of site, from the interconnection of programme, from rational composition and from construction itself. Beauty, therefore, is not an academic code but an amelioration of reality. In this context, Eduardo Souto de Moura works with land, with vegetation, with climate and with an exposed palette of materials to create unique places. But, Souto de Moura also likes to incorporate found fragments – recycled columns, for example – almost as puns so that his new architecture is a form of bricolage or assemblage. The visual is paramount, enticing and unashamed.

Most obvious in the work of Williams and Tsien, with its exploration of many different materials, heterogeneity distinguishes an architecture of slow beauty from strict minimalism. All four practices typically emphasize the innate characteristics of stone, metal and wood, and are attentive to their volumetric display. Witness Kishi's use of luxuriant marble on the upper floor of the house in Higashi-Osaka (p. 64). Chipperfield's interiors for restaurants and boutiques (for example, Dolce & Gabbana on London's Bond Street) are gatherings of such textures, miniature landscapes or sensual topologies. His free-standing designs meanwhile, such buildings as the River and Rowing Museum at Henley-on-Thames, England (p. 32) and a proposed house in Martha's Vineyard off America's East Coast, can be almost reticent on the exterior. Perhaps it is simply rude to draw too much attention to oneself?

It is this mixture of inside and outside, of invention and convention that makes Chipperfield's vast proposal for Berlin's Museuminsel so intriguing. There should be no single photographic opportunity. Beauty in these projects is never one fixed image but rather a complex sensory experience.

Contingent and never exactly ideal, coolness may play a role analogous to that of classical beauty in ancient cultures. Rather than being an issue of style, yet another ism in our generally chaotic postmodern age, cool construction can make one pause, can function to slow things down. This architecture of slow beauty harnesses the time and effort required to realize buildings of substance. It prioritizes the multidimensional experience of architecture and facilitates human response. Slow beauty dwells on the tactile and the spatial – it is both humane and intellectual. These are not works to be ticked off at speed by the insatiable architectural tourist. They demand patience and ease and slow scrutiny. Take your time. Return often.

1   Ricoeur, Paul. Translated, with an introduction, by Charles A. Kelbley. 'Universal Civilization and National Culture'. *History and Truth* (Evanston: Northwestern University Press, 1965)
2   Frampton, Kenneth. *Modern Architecture: A Critical History*. 3rd ed. (London and New York: Thames & Hudson, 1992)
3   Heidegger, Martin. Translated, with introduction, by Albert Hofstadter. *Poetry, Language, Thought* (New York: Harper & Row, 1971)
4   Herbert, Zbigniew. Translated by John and Bogdana Carpenter. *Still Life with a Bridle: Essays and Apocryphas* (Hopewell, NJ: Ecco Press, 1994)

4.00
Neurosciences Institute,
Tod Williams and Billie Tsien
[this page]
Cranbrook Natatorium,
Tod Williams and Billie Tsien
[opposite]

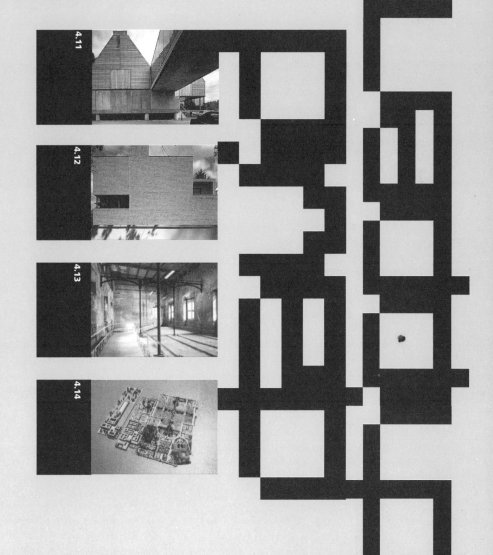

4.11

4.12

4.13

4.14

David Chipperfield
Reciprocity and Logic

Culture is the locus of the search
for lost unity.
Guy Debord[1]

The opening of Issey Miyake's London boutique in 1985 was a cosmopolitan sensation. There was a seductive power about this interior for the Japanese fashion designer: its materiality and spatial manipulation, its planar plaster walls and ceilings, its exposed timber bench and solid-stone floor, its large nude slab of grained white marble. Intended of course for profit, and fashion being inherently ephemeral, there was nevertheless something timeless in the shocking calm of that marble slab. The Miyake boutique was modern in a classic sense, reminiscent of works by such Italian rationalists as Giuseppe Terragni (Italy's interwar avant-garde enjoyed an intellectual revival in the 1980s). Memorable for its cool elementalization, the store was also a small prototypical building.

David Chipperfield's career was founded on such rarefied interior projects.The London venture (realized in collaboration with Ken Armstrong) led to further boutiques for Miyake in Japan, to shops for Equipment and Joseph in Europe, and to a collaboration in 1987 between Chipperfield and artist Bruce McLean for the interior of Bristol's Arnolfini Gallery. This was not the predictable trajectory for an employee of both Richard Rogers and Norman Foster, the twin tsars of English High-Tech. In 1989, Chipperfield interviewed Foster for the Catalan journal *Quaderns*, a question-and-answer session that revealed as much about the younger man as it did about the global superstar. The questioner seemed more interested in the modern possibilities of natural material – timber and stone – than in any space-age technology.

Chipperfield's intimate and contextual designs are unapologetically sensuous. Complexly English, this is an architect who values understatement, who has a practical respect for the past, and who takes professional pleasure from small projects well done. There is something in his work of the bespoke tailor.

As an independent practitioner, Chipperfield moved between careful interiors in the UK and a series of free-standing buildings in Japan. Although physically distant, one can easily understand the English architect's attraction to aspects of Japanese visual culture: its essential use of stone, timber and, more recently, concrete; its layering of constructed and natural elements to create unexpected moments of serenity in confined urban contexts. The mixing together of a rationalist urbanism and Japan's seemingly ethereal, traditional spirit is evident in three mixed-use buildings that Chipperfield realized between 1987 and 1992: the Gotah Private Museum in Tokyo, the Toyota Auto building in Kyoto and the Matsumoto construction company headquarters in the southwest city of Okayama.

Back home, Chipperfield has now inhabited his purpose-built studio in Camden Town for more than a decade. It shares certain sensory aspects with Tadao Ando's concrete work in Japan, but the studio is also engrained in its London setting. It is a fusion of loft and mews typologies with a tough elegance in the texture of components and the manipulation of daylight. Chipperfield's methodology has in part to do with his training at Foster's and Rogers's offices, with their exploration and refinement of how elements of a building go together, how membrane (or skin) and structure can be manipulated for optimal volume – all part of an established trait in English architecture that celebrates engineering prowess. To this, Chipperfield has added observations from his travels and from the realities of everyday life.

These themes in Chipperfield's work have finally been embodied in one building: the River and Rowing Museum (p. 32) at Henley-on-Thames, England. Henley is proof of the architect's ability to construct a complex modern building carefully grafted from the vernacular. A late-twentieth-century centre for the interpretation of history, sport and the environment, Chipperfield's design uses the most up-to-date technology, but does not call undue attention to it. Its tactic is to accept and learn from the normative, from commonly recognizable neighbourhood types, in this case riverside and rural sheds. Henley shares this appreciation of the everyday and contextual with the holiday home Chipperfield is building for himself and his family in northwest Spain. These are perhaps the projects with most personal significance for the architect.

Chipperfield fuses state-of-the-art construction techniques with his own common sense and distilled aesthetic preferences to produce works of architecture that, as in Henley, are evolutionary rather than revolutionary; that, like his house in Germany (p. 38), have complex interpenetrations of solid and void, of matter and light; that, as in the case of the Neues Museum (p. 42) proposal, exploit the coexistence of old and new; and that, like his initial Miyake boutique, are unmistakably beautiful. As with Souto de Moura, his finest work has ambiguity. Chipperfield seems to doubt the apparent certainties of High-Tech, instead accepting and registering impurity and change, allowing – unlike so much recent instantaneous design – for the passing of time.

By the early 1990s, projects in Germany had become central to Chipperfield's career. First he realized a housing precinct in Berlin and a small mixed-use tower along the quays in Düsseldorf. Second, in 1995, he became a professor at the Staatliches Akademie der Bildenden Künste in Stuttgart. Then came the house in Germany. Unlike Chipperfield's earlier residential work (the 1987 house remodel for photographer Nick Knight, for instance, in Richmond, Surrey), the brick villa is neither a refurbishment nor subservient to its context. It is a three-storey, free-standing structure that Chipperfield has approached with vigour and restraint. If the boutiques are memorable for single exquisite swatches of material, the house in Germany is a multidimensional composition enlivened by movement and light. An essay rather than a poem.

Competition successes have followed in quick succession, with first prizes awarded to proposals for Leipzig (Germany), Davenport (Iowa), Venice, Milan and Salerno (all in Italy). Placed second in 1994 with initial ideas for the Neues Museum in Berlin, Chipperfield won a second and decisive competition in 1997. Since then, the architect best know for his interiors has been faced with the prospect of masterplanning the entire museum precinct. When complete, the reorganized Museuminsel, with its several distinct monuments, will be part of the re-presentation of Berlin as a world capital. With Norman Foster's work on the Reichstag, Daniel Libeskind's controversial Jewish Museum and Peter Zumthor's yet-to-be-built 'Topography of Terror', Chipperfield's task is to engage the metropolitan ambitions of Berlin with issues of history, the appropriation of memory and the passing of time.

Why is this architect's practice so entwined with the design of museums and art galleries? From his earliest boutique and renovation projects, Chipperfield has shown an uncanny ability to make interventions that are elegant and striking in themselves but that simultaneously serve as backdrops to the display of fashion or art. His is a kind of reciprocal practice, concerned less with so-called 'signature buildings' than with threading together chains of architectural spaces and events, particular moments that can be tailored to the requirements of curators and merchandisers. If the house in Germany is seen as a single idea impacted by a series of functional and spatial needs, inversely the image of the Museuminsel is arrived at by the accretion of individual solutions, analogous to the layering of time itself.

Chipperfield's office continues to design boutiques (Joseph Menswear on London's Sloane Avenue) and restaurants (Wagamama in Soho, Circus near Golden Square). The smaller projects are consciously used as testing grounds for the larger buildings, as laboratories investigating new techniques, spatial relationships and comfort (an attitude for which Adolf Loos and Eileen Gray provide early modernist antecedents). Chipperfield's concern for volumetric cognition and for sensory pleasure is not part of some grand didactic view of architecture – such an a priori position would contradict his trust in the empirical. Even a project dealing directly with monumentality – the extension of Venice's San Michele Cemetery (p. 46) – avoids the overly emphatic. There in the famous lagoon, new work will complement the old and will reinforce given conditions so that one could not exist without the other.

This then is an architecture that does not overwhelm. The first small renovations, for example, exhibit a willingness and ability to work within a given context or envelope. Now with such bigger new-build projects as the Davenport Museum of Art, a high-rise hotel at Miami Beach and the Salerno Palace of Justice, David Chipperfield must develop strategies that connect architecture to its site at a robust urban scale. With such complex scenarios as the Museuminsel precinct, the architect also needs a panoply of managerial and expert skills. Employees and consultants to some degree bring these abilities to a practice, but it is tempting to surmise that Chipperfield honed an aptitude for large-scale work in his High-Tech days before that single marble slab.

1   Debord, Guy. Translated by Donald Nicholson-Smith. *The Society of the Spectacle* (New York: Zone Books, 1994)

River and Rowing Museum
Henley-on-Thames, England, 1989–96

4.1 Chipperfield's first major work in England, the museum is situated downstream from the famous regatta town of Henley in a flat meadow alongside the Thames. Artifacts that explain the local river ecology and the traditions and contemporary practice of competitive rowing are housed in two parallel containers (one sixteen bays long, the other twelve). Sitting on stout pilotis, the concrete columns favoured by Le Corbusier, these containers are clad in horizontal strips of green oak and lit through contiguous slits in their pitched steel-clad roofs. The lower level is glazed as a highly transparent deck to accommodate entry, a shop and café, offices, services and supplementary exhibition space. A subsidiary wing is tethered to the main building by a concrete bridge, creating a portico entrance to the car park.

The two long containers are reminiscent of rowing-club boathouses and of timber barns found in the English countryside. The materials – concrete, glass, oak, terne-coated steel – have a matter-of-factness about them, an ordinariness even, but are assembled with an elegant attention to proportion, to connections and to surface. The lower deck with its extended stairways and ramps is raised on low concrete legs to float over the flood plain like certain temple or palace structures in ancient Japanese gardens. The in-situ concrete of the bridge, the oak siding carefully pinned by vertical pairs of rivets and the floor-to-ceiling plates of glass on the lower level are flush with each other so that a tautness of form is achieved. Inside, the upper exhibition spaces have high plasterboard ceilings reaching each central spine with its skylight and linear light reflector.

House in Germany
Germany, 1994–96

4.12 This residence in the suburbs of a large German city is a complex exercise in spatial manipulation. It can be understood as a block that has been cut into and eroded to make cubic, patio-like spaces and to allow for the penetration of natural light. Alternatively, it might be described as the unfolding of a brick skin to wrap walls, floors and even the soffits of a succession of rooms that open toward the sun and a large northern garden. The dynamic of the house is introverted and extroverted, reminiscent of early modernist villas by Ludwig Mies van der Rohe (in Krefeld, North Rhine-Westphalia) and the more expressionistic Erich Mendelsohn (in the affluent suburbs west of Berlin). The bricks were all handmade in the former East Germany.

The clients are a couple whose children no longer live at home, who collect contemporary art and who have strict security requirements. The house is screened from the road by an opaque wall behind which a broad flight of brick steps leads up to a double-height vestibule lined in *pietra serena*, a brilliant white stone. Internal stairs rise to the couple's private quarters and descend to an extensive basement that holds a swimming pool designed in collaboration with Los Angeles artist Ed Ruscha. The principal rooms have 13-foot-high (4 metres) ceilings. The drawing room looks north toward the garden, the dining room, library and first-level bedrooms all overlook and gain sunlight from a south-facing courtyard that is walled against the street. A stairway cascades into the rear garden.

Neues Museum

Museuminsel, Berlin, 1996–

4.13 Great nineteenth-century museums are intrinsic to Berlin's cultural heritage. Behind Karl Friedrich Schinkel's Altes Museum, with its stark forecourt facing Unter den Linden, is a cluster of classical buildings on an island in the Spree river. This is Berlin's Museuminsel, a unique precinct that was badly damaged during the Second World War and allowed to deteriorate further under the Communist regime of the DDR. In 1997 and following two design competitions, Chipperfield was asked to remodel Friedrich August Stüler's Neues Museum with its two internal courtyards.

Chipperfield first proposed to erect an independent glass box with a plinth of stone on a highly visible site alongside the river. Examination then focused on the two existing voids within the Neues Museum itself. These damaged courts were to receive grand new staircases (a flat ceremonial one for the Egyptian collection and a more precipitous one for the Greek exhibit) permitting visitors to circulate freely about the structure. This policy of repair and insertion recalls the postwar work of Hans Döllgast in Munich. Finally, Chipperfield decided to sink the courtyard levels and reconstruct one principal staircase in the interstitial hall.

The change of level means that the Neues Museum will be experienced as part of the entire museum quarter. A masterplan directed by Chipperfield (with the firms of Heinz Tesar and Hilmer & Sattler) has now developed the concept of an archeological promenade that links the institutions by a concourse contained within their existing stone bases, a circulation spine invisible from the outside. He proposes to add a single new pristine pavilion along the Spree: a symbolic structure that will help orient visitors and shelter temporary exhibitions. It is intended as the one clear sign of modernization.

Extension to San Michele Cemetery
Venice, 1998

4.14 San Michele has long been the cemetery island for Venice. As the Venetians historically tried to protect what land they had and to colonize outward into the lagoon, the practice occurred of burying citizens away from the city fabric. After many generations of use, it is inevitable that San Michele either intensifies or expands. In his winning 1998 competition entry, David Chipperfield proposes that it do both.

Chipperfield's scheme extends the cemetery's axial geometries to fill an undeveloped corner. Then, with mud made available by dredging, a walled second island will be created, a linear satellite to the original, approached by two short bridges. On both segments of the cemetery, blocklike building will contain a crematorium, chapel and ossuary with burial places along the many wall surfaces and tombstones flush with a central lawn. Rather than an ersatz urbanism (as at Aldo Rossi's famous cemetery in Modena), Chipperfield suggests a connection between the infrastructural and the natural.

It is not uncommon for architects in continental Europe to design cemeteries. In Scandinavia, this activity is traditionally marked by attention to landscape (for example, Asplund and Lewerentz's Stockholm South Cemetery in Sweden, 1918–20). Carlo Scarpa created an exquisite garden grave for the Brion Vega family (1969–78) on the Venetian mainland near Treviso. More recently, Enric Miralles and Carme Pinós have built the extraordinarily tectonic Igualada Cemetery near Barcelona (1985–96). But Chipperfield's proposal is perhaps closest in spirit to that of Luigi Snozzi at Monte Carasso in Ticino: both architects make their architecture one of integration and continuity.

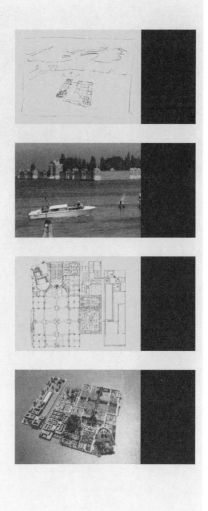

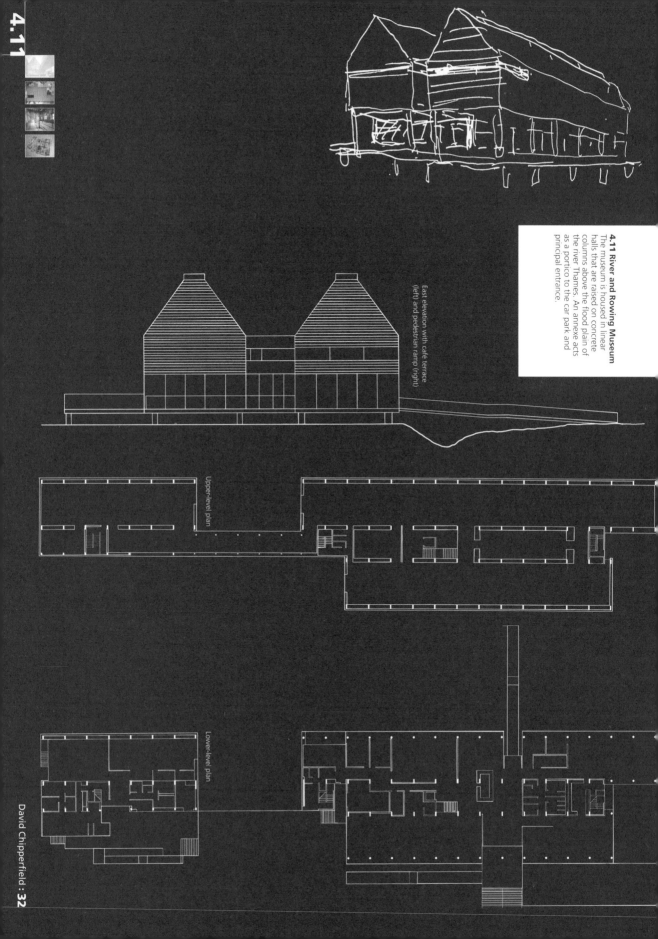

4.11 River and Rowing Museum
The museum is housed in linear halls that are raised on concrete columns above the flood plain of the river Thames. An annexe acts as a portico to the car park and principal entrance.

East elevation with café terrace (left) and pedestrian ramp (right)

Upper-level plan

Lower-level plan

David Chipperfield : **32**

4.11 River and Rowing Museum
The lower level is a glazed envelope, while the upper level is clad in oak and roofed in terne-coated steel. The lower-level exhibition space seems to float amid foliage.

4.11 River and Rowing Museum
A restaurant and terrace are situated on the lower level. Upper exhibition halls have high ceilings, rising to single linear monitors for natural light and artificial lighting fixtures.

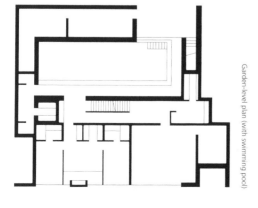

Bedroom-level plan

Entry-level plan (with courtyard)

Garden-level plan (with swimming pool)

South elevation
(toward garden)

North elevation
(toward street)

4.12 House in Germany
Designed in collaboration with Ed Ruscha, the swimming pool on the lower level opens toward a north-facing garden. A double-height entrance hall leads to an internal stairway sequence, off which are all the house's principal rooms.

Longitudinal section
through entry hall
and courtyard

Cross section through
raised courtyard and
pool (right)

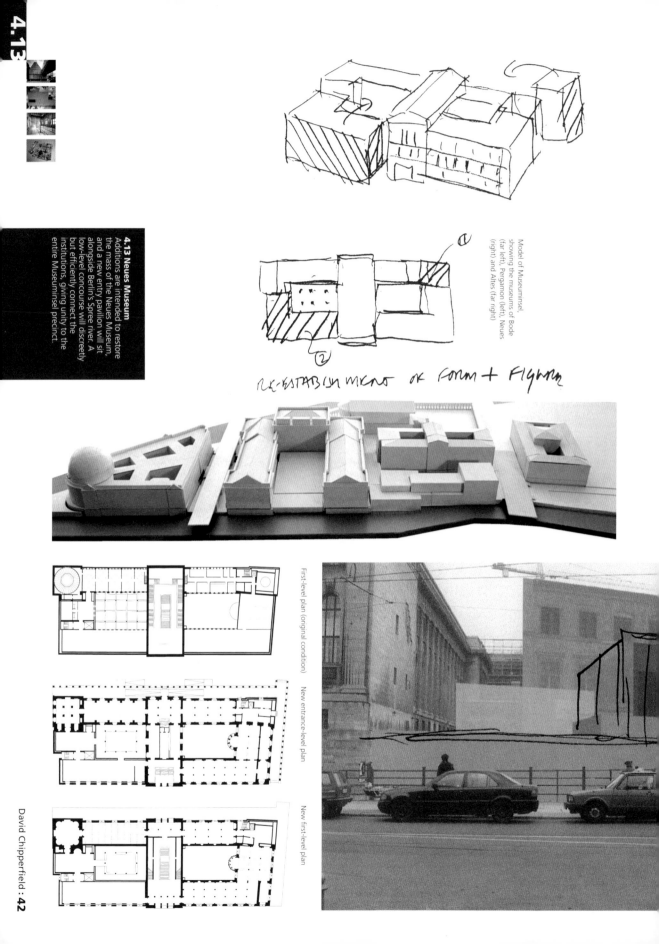

Model of Museuminsel, showing the museums of Bode (far left), Pergamon (left), Neues (right) and Altes (far right)

RE-ESTABLISHMENT OF FORM + FIGURE

4.13 Neues Museum

Additions are intended to restore the mass of the Neues Museum, and a new entry pavilion will sit alongside Berlin's Spree river. A low-level concourse will discreetly but efficiently connect the institutions, giving unity to the entire Museuminsel precinct.

First-level plan (original condition)

New entrance-level plan

New first-level plan

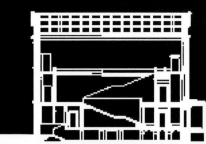

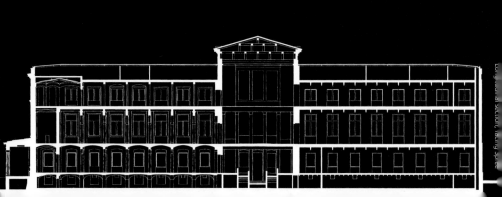

4.13 Neues Museum
Sections show the additions to the perimeter and internal courtyards of the Neues Museum. A single ceremonial stairway will connect all levels of the museum from the tall existing central hallway.

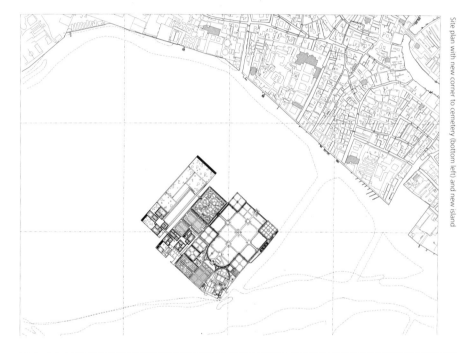

Site plan with new corner to cemetery (bottom left) and new island

4.14 Extension to San Michele Cemetery

The development places new facilities in the corner of the existing island, then creates a new island parallel to the old. The sketch and small photomontage show San Michele's relationship to the city of Venice, and the drawings map out the new families of blocklike forms that have court and garden spaces.

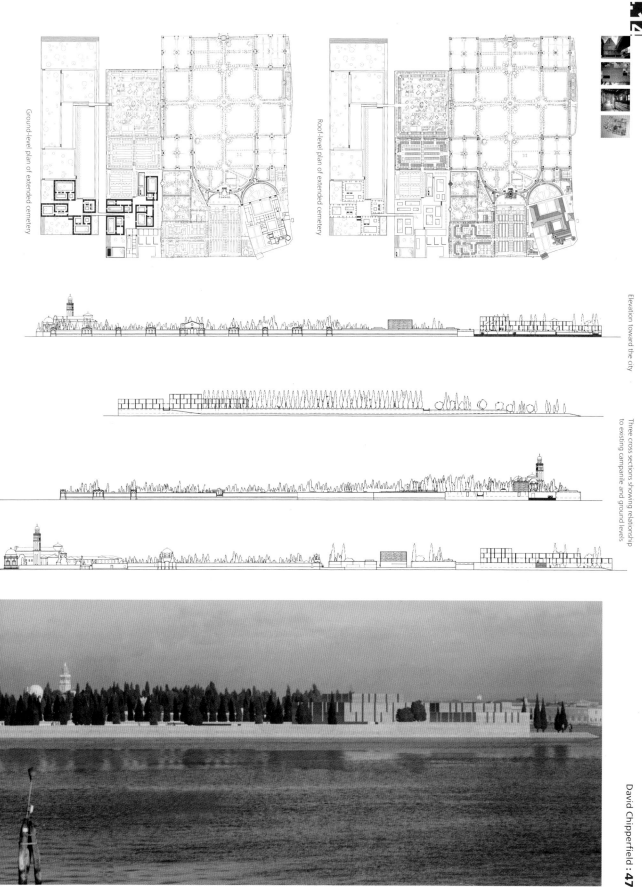

Ground-level plan of extended cemetery

Roof-level plan of extended cemetery

Elevation toward the city

Three cross sections showing relationship to existing campanile and ground levels

David Chipperfield : **47**

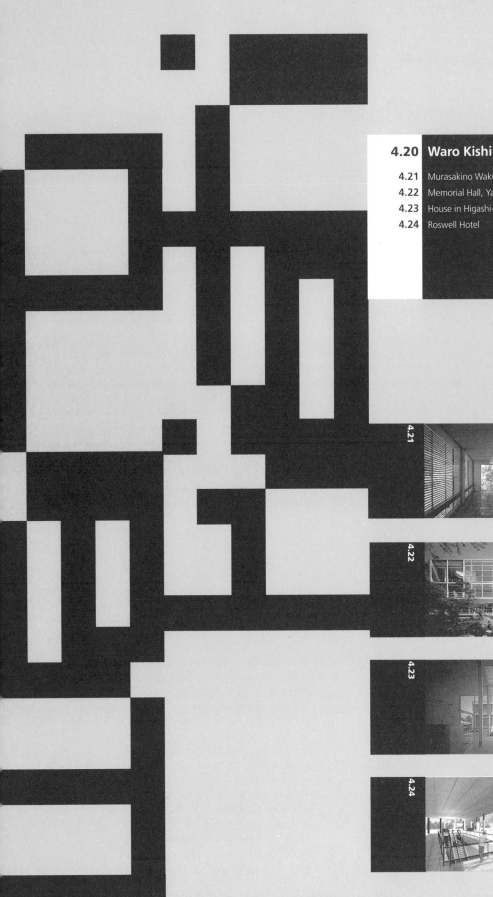

4.20 Waro Kishi

4.21

4.22

4.23

4.24

Waro Kishi

Ideal Appropriations

The sun never knew how wonderful it was
until it fell on the wall of a building.
Louis I. Kahn[1]

Murasakino Wakuden Restaurant (p. 56) stands on
a corner in a northern sector of Kyoto. At first
glance, the restaurant is not particularly inviting: there
is no obvious entrance nor any informative views of the
interior. The unobservant may even dismiss the largely
opaque tower as some kind of utility substation. A more
critical glance, however, reveals a surprising quality and
precision in the vertical planes of concrete, the lower
limestone walls (splayed and incised) and the flush
timber slats above (which screen twin recessed picture
windows). The more one observes and uses this
meticulous project by Waro Kishi, the more one
appreciates the appropriateness of his architecture.

The restaurant faces the Daitoku-ji temple complex.
Chestnut louvres, immediately outside Kishi's first-storey
lunchroom, forbid any voyeuristic view of the ancient
precinct opposite. Conversely, they also permit glimpses
or hints of the temple's forecourt, its palisades and
foliage seep into the calm restaurant space. It is not an
exaggeration to say that one is in a realm of light and
shadows, of subtle textures and natural sensations.
The food is delicious, the illumination discreet. The
unmistakable modernity of Kishi's architecture also
includes or re-presents orthodox Japanese items: a
solid-timber post on a stone base in the entry hall;
a recess like the traditional *tokonoma* alcove with
a sapling column behind the counter upstairs.

To many Westerners, the existence of blatantly new
architecture in such close proximity to subtle treasures
from the past seems anomalous. Blunt adjacency is,
nevertheless, symptomatic of the contemporary
Japanese city, of the sites where Kishi normally builds.
He accepts the limitations of these sites, but moreover
fuses Western and Japanese concepts of space –
particularly interior space – so that both traditions
are refreshed.

Within the Modern Movement, architects were
prone to extracting, judiciously, themes from classic
Japanese sites. Walter Gropius – the key figure at
Germany's Bauhaus in the 1920s and subsequently at
Harvard's Graduate School of Design in the 1930s –
visited Kyoto in the 1950s and the then almost forgotten
palace of Katsura. He reinterpreted in a functionalist

way its decks and screens, its structural and modular
systems, and its connection to nature. Gropius admired
the precise asymmetry and strategic use of contrast in
traditional Japanese settings. He wrote that 'beauty
… is still a basic requirement of life for the Japanese'
and that in Japan, design consisted not of 'aesthetic
abstractions' but of 'meaningful realities related to
daily life'.[2]

For Kishi's generation, therefore, modernism is not
a wholly foreign import. In Japan today, design has
furthermore been influenced by the attempts of such
pioneering figures of the 1950s as Junzo Sakakura and
Kunio Mayekawa to fuse international and indigenous
forms. Kishi's seminal Memorial Hall (p. 60), at Ube in
the far west of Japan, is a refined and vitreous box that
hovers above a much older garden. Unmistakably new,
the building enters into a dialogue with the garden so
that one provides the other with an aesthetic charge.
In the cool glazed skin and floating terrace of the
Memorial Hall, there is a suggestion of early projects by
Gropius and by his colleague Mies van der Rohe; in the
proportions and more plastic interior space, there
is a memory of Le Corbusier's assemblages from the
same period.

The lowest level of the Memorial Hall is half-inside,
half-outside. The lobby has a protective glass membrane
through which light and views flow. The implied
parallelepiped of the primary box form is eaten into,
mixing further the interior and exterior worlds, while
the deck continues outward as a right-angled boardwalk
that colonizes or appropriates the garden. If, at
Yamaguchi, Kishi's expansion of space with its
interpenetration of inside/outside volumes is reminiscent
of planar strategies from the 1920s (Mies van der Rohe's
Brick Villa project, for instance, and designs by the Dutch
De Stijl group), the pleasure in circulation – out above
the garden surface and in along the ceremonial ramp
that connects all three levels – recalls the architectural
promenades of Le Corbusier.

This theme of interlocking space recurs throughout
Kishi's work: at Yamaguchi (where the cubic porch seems
indebted to Le Corbusier's Esprit Nouveau pavilion of
1925), with the extruded masses of the House in
Nakagyo, and even in the tiny entry courtyard of
Murasakino Wakuden. With these staggered plans,

there is an echo of Western avant-garde manoeuvres and a memory of traditional Japan, a mix that is essential to Kishi's work. Gropius commented on the 'favorite Zen approach, which is rarely direct, axial, and symmetrical'. Kishi has referred – in perhaps the same breath as a discussion of Corbusien 'phenomenal transparency' – to the traditional concept of *engawa* or intermediate space, the purpose of which is to make thresholds, moments of delicate definition and redirection.

The Memorial Hall, like Kishi's Kyoto-Kigaku Research Institute at Kansai Science City (1987–90) and his SD office building on the outskirts of Sonobe (1991–93), is able to expand horizontally and to manipulate generously vistas and the admission of natural light. Most of his other realized projects are forced by contextual restrictions to operate in the vertical direction. In the architect's mind, the horizontal realm is associated with the rational (the functionalist adherence to plan and planning), whereas the vertical is connected to emotions and desire. In this respect, Kishi shares some of the phenomenological concerns of the French philosopher Gaston Bachelard. The modern home, Bachelard wrote in the mid-twentieth century, 'has become mere horizontality'.[3]

One can appreciate this sensory opening upward and outward in the exquisite houses Kishi has built on narrow infill sites in the conurbations of Kyoto, Osaka and Kobe. His house in Nipponbashi (1990–92), which first brought the architect to international attention, has a mere 8.2-foot (2.5 metres) frontage. Inside, lower levels have deliberately low floor-to-ceiling heights, an almost Mannerist compression of space that invites a psychological release as one ascends into the tall, thin living room, a sky pavilion above the city streets. His later house in Higashi-Nada (1995–97), a suburb of Kobe, is an elongated concrete box with a 10.8-foot (3.3 metres) street elevation. The family room, with its long central kitchen unit, is discovered on the second floor, the architectural promenade continuing up along a very gently inclined stairway to an outdoor roof terrace.

The daily drama of these houses is not predetermined by remote architectural abstraction. Through geometric expansion and the careful selection of materials, Kishi makes the most of his walls and spaces by setting up visual connections through the building mass itself and by allowing precious glimpses of nature (the enclosed patio tree at Higashi-Osaka [p. 64], a narrow park across the road from Higashi-Nada). 'Something pure', wrote the Japanese composer Toru Takemitsu, 'becomes interesting only when it is combined with something coarse.'[4] Kishi's work is never hermetically sealed in on itself. Instead, the architect engenders a certain life in his buildings by incorporating aspects of the outside world, whether as views or as unexpected components of construction.

A desire for compositional or visual order operates in tandem with Kishi's sense of construction. For all the obvious infiltration of twentieth-century influences and alongside the indigenous hybridization, it is useful to know that Kishi was educated first as an electrical engineer, then as an architectural historian. He seems to pursue a certain truthfulness to structure (poured-in-place concrete, exposed steel sections) and appliances (might the industrial light fittings at Nipponbashi be kin to the car headlights appropriated by Richard Neutra for the Lovell House in Los Angeles of 1927–29?), but he is also an expert on Brunelleschi and the Italian Renaissance. Indeed his favourite method of presentation – orthogonal planes on backgrounds of solid colour – has some of the stillness of early classicism.

Kishi's control of composition, one might almost say his painterly eye, ensures that his architecture is never a simple matter of nuts and bolts. Like Souto de Moura, particularly at Santa Maria do Bouro, Kishi may or may not reveal actual details of construction, for example, the juncture of posts and beams. The visual integrity of his spaces and the way in which they are framed or delineated is paramount. Attentive to reality and everyday life, Kishi is also drawn to abstraction, to a cool idealism. A white steel frame physically and visually structures the site of the House in Shimagamo (1992–94). About and above an encaged void, similar to a traditional *nakaniwa*-type courtyard, the architect spins surfaces of cement panel, clear glass, marble and white plaster into a lucid entity. Similarly, the house in Higashi-Osaka is assembled so that each element of construction participates in a multidimensional tableau.

In *In Praise of Shadows*, Jun'ichiro Tanizaki wrote that 'whiteness (is) … indispensable to supreme beauty'.[5] In Kishi's architecture, whiteness is present in many varied tones, the innate whiteness of marble or plaster, whiteness applied as paint or industrial coating. Whereas in the recent Bus Stop mall boutiques he uses discreet blocks of cadmium yellow, for Kishi white seems to symbolize not the absence of particular things but their unadorned presence, their apotheosis almost. He might be said to have raised family living space to the highest of architectural categories.

1 Kahn, Louis I. Wurman, Richard Saul, ed. *What Will Be Has Always Been: the Words of Louis I. Kahn* (New York: Rizzoli, 1986)
2 Gropius, Walter. *Architettura in Giappone* (Milan: Görlich, 1965)
3 Bachelard, Gaston. Translated by Maria Jolas. *The Poetics of Space* (Boston: Beacon Press, 1969)
4 Takemitsu, Toru. *The Film Music of Toru Takemitsu*, sleeve notes, (Nonesuch 79404, 1997)
5 Tanizaki, Jun'ichiro. Translated by J. Harper and Edward G. Seidensticker. *In Praise of Shadows* (London: Cape, 1991)

Murasakino Wakuden Restaurant

Kyoto, Japan, 1994–95

4.21

At a traffic intersection in Kyoto, this small concrete tower functions as a traditional Japanese restaurant. To the south of the building is a broad avenue with the paraphernalia of contemporary urban life (road signs, overhead power lines, commercial advertisements). Across the calmer street to the west is the Daitoku-ji temple complex, an ancient labyrinth of fenced precincts, moss gardens, timber decks and carefully framed vistas.

Kishi's project harnesses its context in many subtle, almost subordinate, ways. The tower comes forward flush to the avenue, thus creating a tall entrance court with foliage in the resultant void to the north. Its base is splayed in section, like Old Kyoto's 'slanted wooden grilles' of which Walter Gropius wrote. A street-level hallway, used as a pick-up point for the restaurant's lunch-box service, has earthen floors and walls so that what from the outside may at first appear somewhat brutalist or minimalist is revealed, inside, as a surprisingly sensory environment.

Up a dark timber stairway that lies to the rear of the court is the restaurant's lunchcounter. With an expansive view back into the court, the prospect of the temple complex across the street is screened by external chestnut louvres. Interior partitions have chamfered jambs and precisely positioned swatches of protective paper, as in traditional construction. A suspended ceiling with recessed lighting floats over the counter, and the deep-red chairs are made by a craftsman originally apprenticed to the Danish master Hans Wegner.

The kitchen is upstairs on the second level, topped off by a subtly pitched pyramidal roof that is barely perceptible from the exterior.

Memorial Hall
Yamaguchi University, Ube, Japan, 1994–97

4.22 This generous three-storey structure transforms a long-established garden at Yamaguchi University. The pavilion seems to float above the ground. It sends a timber boardwalk out across a traditional Japanese micro-landscape (with its pond, trees and strategically placed rocks), so Kishi's intervention may be considered as a geometric device for the enjoyment of nature. The adjacent campus is much less bucolic: the Memorial Hall opens up toward the south and diverts attention away from a car park, neighbouring residential units and a roadway. It has exposed concrete flanking walls, wooden floors and large expanses of glass to the north and south. Steel columns, window frames, a free-standing staircase and delicate railings are all painted white.

The Memorial Hall serves as a venue for the medical faculty's alumni association and as a small conference centre. Visitors approach the building either across a pool of gravel to pierce its east-facing flank or, more sensually, along the boardwalk from which the expansive ground-level lobby is clearly visible. They then turn at right angles to enter the envelope of the pavilion, into a triple-height open loggia with a staircase and an oculus cut from its ceiling. Solar and visual protection is provided by thin steel grilles to the south and timber slats to the west. An internal ramp extends across much of the north elevation to give ceremonial access to meeting rooms on the upper levels. The south-facing curtain wall is translucent, its proportions suggesting those of Le Corbusier's Villa Stein at Garches (1927).

House in Higashi-Osaka
Osaka, Japan, 1995–97

4.23 In a typically dense Japanese neighbourhood with many railway lines and overhead cables, this house maximizes the volume of its site and filters light through external and internal skins. It is an introverted dwelling but also delicate, energetic and reminiscent of a multidimensional x-ray.

Kishi has erected a triple-storey white steel cage to frame the entire site. This skeletal device is three bays deep, two bays wide and has a shallower bay in front to negotiate between the privacy of the home and the public street. Most of the back portion of the house is left as a void with southwestern exposure to sunlight, a single tree, and open-tread steel stairs leading from enclosed rooms below to an expansive living space above.

Above the living area – a rather pristine loft, floored in a lightly grained white marble – the frame expands upward so that it is one-and-a-half-bays high. It is indicative of the architect's willingness to adapt his purist or mathematical interests to empirical conditions. This expansion of the frame allows the spatial impression of the project to be more generous and complex.

Kishi's ease with architectural assemblage is visible on the exterior façade, where fixed and sliding, opaque and translucent, grille and mesh panels coexist. One segment of the roof is made from translucent panels, intensifying the visual interpenetration of the upper volumes. Kishi's use of often modular, ready-to-build components is symptomatic of his concern for 'the industrial vernacular', for an engagement with the actual or the ordinary.

Roswell Hotel

Roswell, New Mexico, 1997

Soon after his 1997 competition proposal for the Kansai regional branch of Japan's National Library, Kishi embarked upon a second monumental competition task, this time for a hotel in the unusual setting of Roswell, New Mexico. His design of a sleek fourteen-storey slab exhibits both the heritage of twentieth-century modernism and an almost geological or topographic character.

The hotel makes no pretence to replicate the pueblo architecture of the American Southwest. Bedrooms are stacked in linear chains, high above an adjacent park and the City Hall, with open corridors like the modernist idea of streets in the air. The slab sits above a semi-interred basement level that shelters conference halls and larger public facilities, then curves inward to offer views and create a distinctively sinuous mass. The two long flanks are sheathed in horizontal louvres, aluminium on the east, frosted glass on the west, inducing physical, climatic and psychological protection between inner and outer worlds.

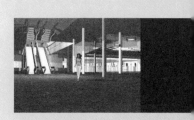

The filigreed or stacked nature of Kishi's proposal is distinct from the typically condensed hive of modern hotels. The fact that his corridors are one-sided increases their engagement with light and the outdoors. Ground- and penthouse levels are opened up and articulated as shaded communal zones – a play on classical architecture's base, middle and top. With a 147.6-foot (45 metres) roof datum borrowed from an immediate neighbour, Kishi's design is a linear extrusion that changes direction in plan like a glacier or mesa form. The architect also proposed inserting one vertical chasm within the mass, and peeling back one horizontal strip in the skin, thus introducing a sense of scale and grandeur.

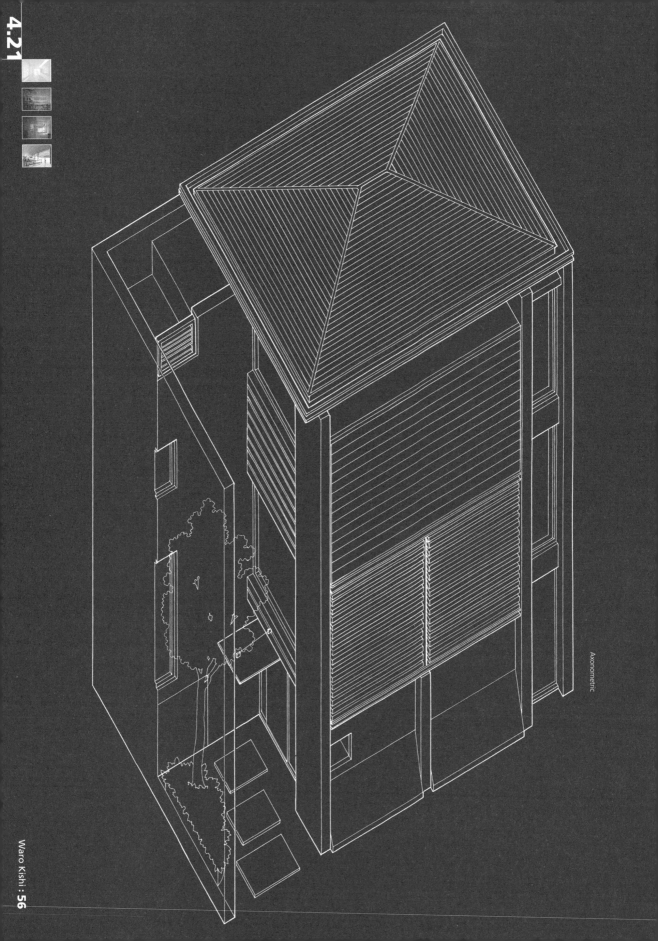

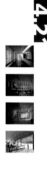

4.21 Murasakino Wakuden Restaurant
The seating area of this small restaurant inhabits the middle level of a three-storey tower. The concrete building is placed at the exact corner of its urban site, with a tall garden entrance away from the traffic intersection. Services are in the zone against the longer part of the wall.

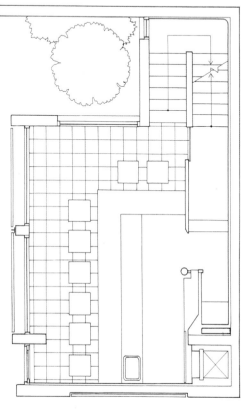

First-level plan

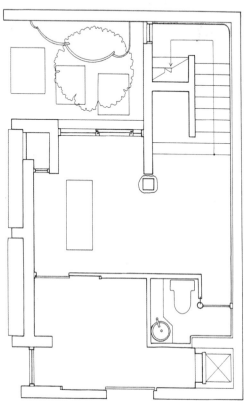

Ground-level plan

4.21 Murasakino Wakuden Restaurant

The entry level is introverted. Natural materials are used and traditional objects are placed in a contemporary setting. The middle-level restaurant has an L-shaped counter with a suspended ceiling, and views toward the temple precinct are veiled by a timber lattice.

Cross section with existing temple complex

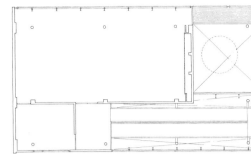

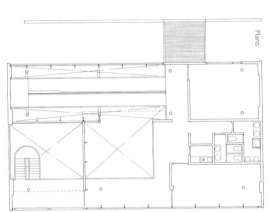

Plans

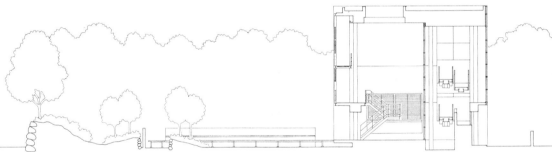

Longitudinal section

4.22 Memorial Hall, Yamaguchi University
A ramp with open railing links all three levels. Opaque glass at the upper levels screens the interior from the existing Japanese garden. Using up-to-date construction techniques, the hall's plan and section recall Le Corbusier's designs of the 1920s.

**4.22 Memorial Hall,
Yamaguchi University**
A triple-height void beyond the
main lounge contains an industrial-
style stairway and walkways, and is
illuminated through a circular cut in
the ceiling. The hall's lower levels
are double-height spaces, with the
ramp visible to the right and the
garden views across a shaded
veranda to the left.

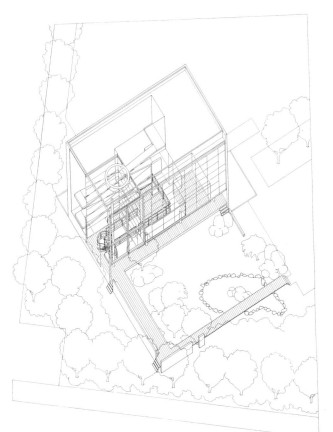

Axonometric

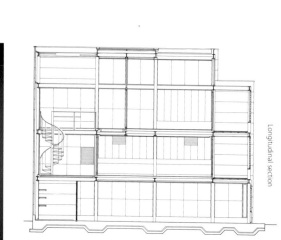

Longitudinal section

Ground-level plan

4.23 House in Higashi-Osaka

The building presents a semi-opaque façade to the street, with edited glimpses of shallow front terraces and internal stairs. The Tatami room at ground level looks into the courtyard, which contains a solitary tree and where an open-tread stairway leads to a spiral staircase between the middle and upper levels.

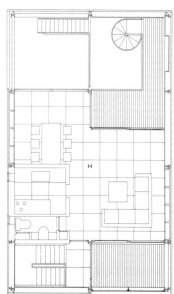

Second-level plan

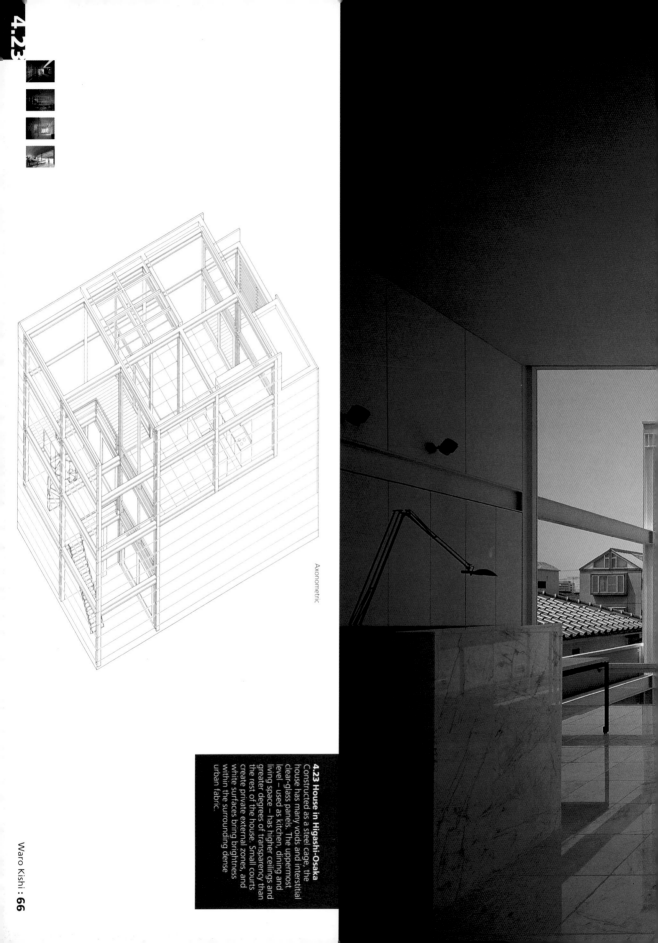

Axonometric

4.23 House in Higashi-Osaka
Constructed as a steel cage, the house has many voids and interstitial clear-glass panels. The uppermost level – used as kitchen, dining and living space – has higher ceilings and greater degrees of transparency than the rest of the house. Small courts create private external zones, and white surfaces bring brightness within the surrounding dense urban fabric.

4.24 Roswell Hotel
This proposal was envisaged as a cranked linear building with walkways open to the sky, to lateral views and to communal spaces for the hotel guests. The building mass was eroded to create volumetric incidents on a grand scale. The east skin is made from aluminium, the west from glass.

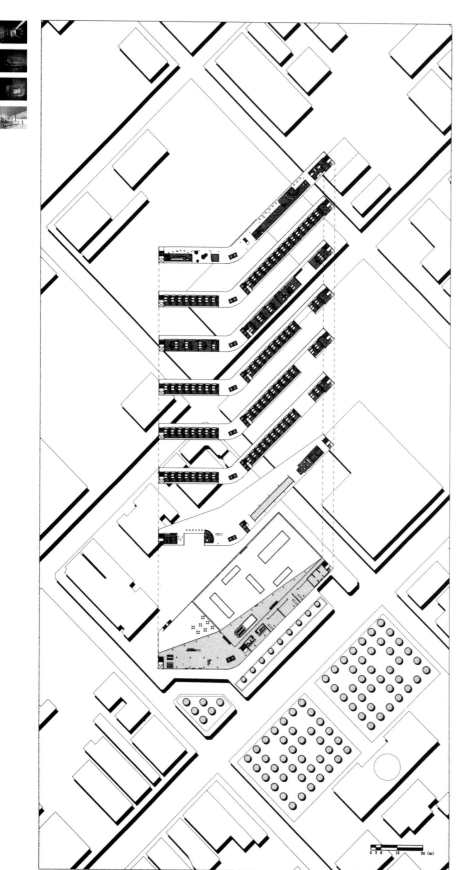

4.24 Roswell Hotel

The rooms are aligned to overlook City Hall and the park, then turn at the elevator lobbies to show more distant views and to embrace the public space below. Escalators connect the street-level foyer with lower-level facilities, including a conference suite.

Exploded site plan

0 3 6   15   30 (m)

Eduardo Souto de Moura
Freedom of the Abstract

I've always disliked the division between form
and content and have never known what to
answer when asked 'but what is the content?',
'what does it mean?'.
Donald Judd (Yale lecture, September 1983)[1]

With the simplest of shapes, Eduardo Souto de Moura
creates architecture that often appears almost entirely
empty. The sparse, geometric envelopes of his buildings
open up to sunlight and sky and occasionally to nature.
His work is marked by a pursuit of ideals that are made
particular by their engagement with Portuguese reality.

Part of a rich architectural culture in Porto, Souto
de Moura is a younger colleague of Fernando Tavora
(Porto's statesman) and Alvaro Siza Vieira (winner of the
international Pritzker Prize in 1992). All three architects
share a studio building designed by Siza, near the high-
spanning Arrábida bridge over the river Douro. Souto
de Moura is not stylistically a regionalist – he does not
regurgitate traditionalist imagery or form – but his work
is enriched by close observation of local building practice
and by dialogue, collaboration even, with these
experienced architects. Although each man pursues
his own individual strand of design, they learn from
each other and from the world in which they live.

Souto de Moura is interested in such radical art
movements as Italian arte povera, with its re-
presentation of everyday materials, and minimalism
as developed in New York from the 1960s onward.
He is simultaneously attracted to modern literature,
to certain Portuguese writers and to the rigorous if
caustic Austrian master Thomas Bernhard (1931–89).
Souto de Moura's buildings, therefore, share the distilled
formality and careful placement of objects from these
art movements with the wit and balance of his favourite
writers. Produced by both hand and mind, each of the
Porto architect's many realized works has a clear
essence, a kind of lean, often paradoxical spirit divined
from programme, site, material construction and from
the designer's own predilections toward abstraction.

At only twenty-five years of age, the architect
designed his first solo project: a minuscule holiday cabin
in the Portuguese National Park of Gerês, a splendid
landscape not far from Santa Maria do Bouro, the
monastery he was later to reconstruct as a hotel (p. 80).

The holiday cabin represents a smooth synthesis of
archaic fragments and new concepts of cool, extensive
space. In the middle of the eighteenth century, the Abbé
Laugier wrote of the Primitive Hut, an essential unit of
habitation emerging from the wild to become the origin
of entire styles and systems. The ersatz ruin at Gerês,
with its sliding glass façade and simple living space that
opens up to nature is Souto de Moura's Primitive Hut.
Although the building is tiny, almost invisible, and far
from the city, it continues to be an archetype for the
architect's work.

Gerês led to the house at Baião where ruins have
been incorporated as bookends that support a clean
expanse of new glazed space, a ruse never attempted
by Mies van der Rohe, and a method that was recently
employed in a house at Moledo (1991–97), where the
rear glass wall is exposed to a fissure of raw rock. At
Baião, the glass curtain rises past the edge of the
roof slab so that visually the entire construction
dematerializes against the hillside. At Moledo,
overlooking the Atlantic near the border with Galicia,
the roof is a single deck beneath which the house is
accommodated. It is a datum with chimney and service
outlets variously boxed as a three-dimensional still life.
The integration of abstract form and space is manifest at
an institutional scale at Porto's Casa das Artes (1981–91),
a cultural centre with walls of different materials that
slide past each other to blend with an existing garden.

Souto de Moura's attention to space as the primary
matter of architecture may in part be a response to the
high population densities found in central Porto, but it
is also a continuation of the historic European ambition
to achieve a form of transcendence through the
idealization of space itself. Such an idealization has
a resonance today for architects and sculptors. For
example, sculptor Donald Judd's boxes in steel or
concrete and his vituperative comments about the
irrelevancy of much contemporary design, appeal to the
architect. Judd's sculptures share a reduced geometric
elegance with Souto de Moura's 'table-top' houses,
where roof and flank walls are homogeneous,
conceptually equal planes, and where siting is
meticulously judged. For the Bom Jesus house (1989–97)
near Braga, the table top gains legs or side walls to sit
subtly on top of the inhabited ashlar plinth.

In larger urban projects, Souto de Moura has absorbed the lessons of Italian neo-rationalists, especially the poetic methodology of Aldo Rossi. Thus, his covered market for Braga (1980–84) is a minimalist construction with its own autonomous typology inserted into a rather frayed, edge-of-city situation. In these early works, one experiences directly the clarity of form and structure adjusted to circumstance that is the hallmark of Souto de Moura's architecture. Later projects planned for more suburban or less tissued sites, such as the Rua do Teatro Apartments in Porto (p. 86) and the Department of Geosciences at Aveiro University, achieve the romantic object quality admired by Rossi by stacking repeated elements of construction within a clearly defined box-form or parallelepiped. At Aveiro, the architect's furniture floats as exquisite boxes above polished-slate floors.

Rossi was concerned with history and continuity: Souto de Moura's buildings incorporate the past and are unmistakably modern. This inclusion of the past – as evidenced by fragments of columns and cut stone – is symptomatic of the ease felt by members of the School of Porto toward heritage and toward the vernacular. You can see in Souto de Moura's simplest sketches a concern for site, a few lines meeting or overlapping to define a place of settlement. This, then, is not a dogmatic modernism existing on its own tabula rasa. Nor is it concerned with postmodern semiotics, with eclectic quotations. Souto de Moura is too much at home in his world and too astute to attempt to dictate any codifiable reading. His aim is to colonize sites with floors, walls and ceilings, to harness or frame their particular characteristics. Form and content are co-dependent.

The reduction of architecture to horizontal and vertical planes was of course an early modernist trademark, a modus operandi of the Russian suprematists, the Dutch De Stijl group and Mies van der Rohe at the Bauhaus. Unlike the Dutch, whose plastic and utopian compositions appeared independent of place, Souto de Moura works with his sites so that the pre-existing and newly built combine symbiotically. His architecture treats the ground and the vegetation almost as ingredients of collage, architecture as a form of installation. The courtyard houses at Matosinhos seem

interred. At the pousada of Santa Maria do Bouro, the roof has been grassed so as to settle into the landscape. Existing fragments of architecture have been adjusted and relocated in a way quite different from orthodox archeology.

There is a sophisticated beauty in the materials that Souto de Moura uses, but techniques are not always on view. At the pousada he includes broad planks of Chilean pine for upper-level corridors, Cor-Ten ceilings, oxidized or patinated copper doors and blocks of red Verona marble that act as isolated stepping stones. These interventions are clearly recent but do not scream their newness. In Thomas Bernhard's novel *Extinction*, the narrator berates his aristocratic family for its unwillingness to explore the unproved or unclassified. 'Everything new', Bernhard wrote, 'is utterly despised and detested ... new houses, new churches, new roads, new inventions and of course new people. To everything new, in fact, including of course new ideas.'[2] Souto de Moura is neither afraid of the new nor disparages the past. He uses contemporary methods and forms boldly, but it is not his aim to be revolutionary. The key parts of his projects are often invisible.

This is in part the cool ambiguity of Souto de Moura's architecture. It is in the vanguard of modernism yet also a kind of camouflage, nestling into its setting. It tends to be a strict geometric construct yet it fosters spatial and conceptual fluidity. This concurrently sharp and soft architecture is perhaps most manifest in the unrealized Burgo Tower (p. 94) proposed for Porto's Avenida da Boavista. Souto de Moura's design for an office building was a repeated rectangular plan stacked through eighteen storeys, a massing that normally produces yet another fixed box on the urban skyline. The Burgo Tower, however, suggests something much more intriguing: with elevations made up of stacked elements, three horizontal modules per floor, its scale becomes difficult to determine. There is a switching back and forth between transparent and opaque elements on alternate façades.

This new ethic of accretion suggests an environmental construct, modulating according to light, rather than any instantly classifiable static object. In this sense, Souto de Moura is very different from Rossi. He is consistently concerned with matters of construction. With Burgo, one might say that content has itself become form.

1   *Donald Judd. Complete Writings 1975–1986* (Eindhoven: Van Abbemuseum, 1987)
2   Bernhard, Thomas. Translated by David McLintock. *Extinction: A Novel* (Chicago: University of Chicago Press, 1996)

Pousada Santa Maria do Bouro

Braga, Portugal, 1989–97

4.31

Pousadas are hotels run by the Portuguese government that are usually on sites of natural or historic interest. Near the National Park of Gerês, an enchanting landscape of forests and mountain streams, Santa Maria do Bouro was a medieval monastery closed down by the Liberal authorities in the 1830s. The church and its twin campanile remains in place above a flight of mossy flagstones. What were the principal monastic dwellings, arranged orthogonally about a cloister and a courtyard with orange trees to the south, have been restructured by Souto de Moura with a modernist elegance. The materials on view, waiting to be touched, include broad timber panels, large sheets of glass, oxidized copper and red marble.

Organized about broad first-level corridors, bedrooms look out across the pousada's terraces to a small swimming pool and the agriculturally fecund valley below. Each room contains a bathroom that is like a large walk-in closet. Beds face outward to the original window openings, now meticulously filled with single metal-framed panes of glass. The architect has added several amusing touches (a folded mirror that conceals a private bar, a jaunty tray-on-wheels) with an attitude that is not slavishly devoted to either minimalism or historical correctness. His wit is also evident in the communal spaces below, where new exposed blocks of marble lead, as if pieces in a clever board game, from one space to the next and walls retain the temporary lettering used by stonemasons.

The restaurant has a horizontal opening mysteriously cut into the ancient walls. In the evenings, a flaming fireplace suffuses the air with a delicate fragrance.

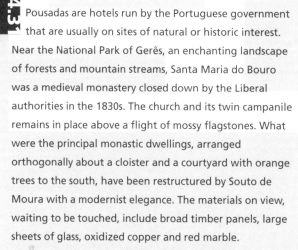

Rua do Teatro Apartments
Matosinhos, near Porto, Portugal, 1992–95

4.32 This bipartite apartment block sits on an eclectic and gently sloping street in Matosinhos, a seaside suburb of Porto. By shunting one segment of massing back from the other, the architect mitigates its impact upon the pavement. The ground level shelters a retail store and entrance foyer; it also provides car access to a basement garage and pedestrian access to a shared rear garden. A typical floor has two large apartments separated by, and staggered about, the communal hall and elevator core. Furthermore, the building is staggered in profile – it is one storey higher as it comes forward to meet the street. Both apartments at the top of the building rise through two storeys with terraces offering fine views toward the Atlantic.

The aesthetic of the street façade is reminiscent of mid-twentieth-century projects inspired by Mies van der Rohe. Its steel framework is expressed externally, painted white and infilled with generous glazing. The rear façade is, however, panelled with ribbed metal sheeting and horizontal windows. The short side elevations are clad in slate, hung to a locally common fish-scale pattern.

Inside, the apartments' living spaces open up through floor-to-ceiling glass toward the sea. Walls and ceilings are uniformly white, while floors are a deep-red tropical wood. The structural frame continues through the building, with one free-standing steel column in each apartment. Souto de Moura has customized the columns by inlaying a single strip of mirror: a witty homage to sculptor Donald Judd and intended for knotting ties.

4.33

Courtyard Housing
Matosinhos, near Porto, Portugal, 1993

Comprising nine almost identical units, plus one free-standing house, this development at Matosinhos is planted in the former vegetable garden of a very grand villa. The courtyard residences exist in a context that is at once arcadian and heavily industrial: the garden suggests themes of geometry and the pleasures of nature, whereas views to the adjacent harbour of Porto de Leixões show working cranes and ocean-going container vessels that firmly connect the luxurious realm of the houses to the reality of the everyday.

The local authority has proposed to drive a new road across the property, dividing the site into a major, trapezoidal section and a minor, triangular one (this small triangle is home to the single individual house). The trapezoid has been sliced by parallel walls so that the plot might be described as ten walls defining nine lots, with three horizontal roof planes overlaid at right angles. One stagger in the plan, allowing for the diagonal road, results in five lots each large enough to accommodate a swimming pool.

Beneath the roofs, the interior is planned by using a system of secondary orthogonal walls. Lowered ceilings lead from the initial bedroom area past a completely internalized courtyard to living spaces with a panoramic prospect of the rear garden beyond. Bedrooms are gathered about a skylight. Souto de Moura has also designed several pieces of furniture (a console cabinet, for instance, that juts into the main living space) as dynamic interior components.

Burgo Tower
Porto, Portugal, 1991

The Avenida da Boavista leads west in a straight line from the Praça da Republica in central Porto to the affluent suburb of Nevogilde and the beach at Matosinhos. Just before this major thoroughfare crosses the motorway that encircles the city proper, several large building blocks are being developed. In 1991, Souto de Moura explored the possibilities of building an eighteen-storey office tower with an adjacent four-storey annexe on a crisp orthogonal podium. As the principal volumetric and structural criteria had already been determined by other consultants, the architect focused on the construction of the building's façades.

The elevations were in part inspired by the stacks of stone and timber found near quarries and lumber mills throughout northern Portugal. The taller tower was to have its narrower north and south façades made of horizontal granite bands separated by thin slots of glass and protruding boxes of steel. The wider façades reversed that formula, with large expanses of glass (some operable) recessed within a regular steel frame. Souto de Moura proposed three such modules between every floor, with the lowermost panel over a concrete lip wall used to screen services.

The attention to the stacking of building elements proved very effective in the Department of Geosciences Building at Aveiro University, where horizontal louvres of vermilion stone screen a three-storey volume. Unlike the mundane towers – derived loosely from the Modern Movement – of today's international business districts, the Burgo project promises to be a metropolitan artifact with a remarkable filigreed and sensuous character.

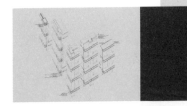

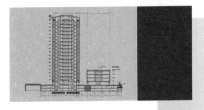

Third-level plan

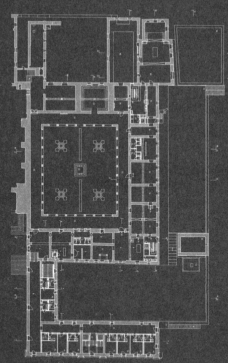

Second-level plan

First-level plan

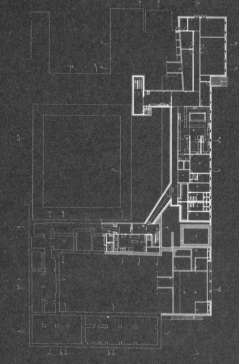

Ground-level plan

4.31 Pousada Santa Maria do Bouro
The historic site consists of a church (still in use) and previously abandoned stone buildings that line one entirely enclosed courtyard, with another open to landscape and trees below. Twin church towers and the former kitchen chimney (right) stand out from the forest surroundings.

**4.31 Pousada Santa Maria
do Bouro**
Sharing a forecourt with the church,
the pousada is entered at right angles
under an archway that also leads to
an orange-tree court. The restaurant,
in part beneath the chimney, has a
new horizontal viewing window
above the water basin on the upper
terrace; stairs lead to the circular
swimming pool below

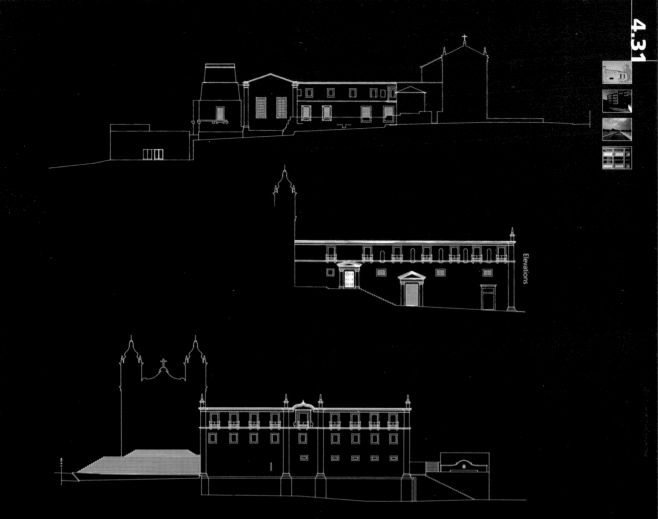

Elevations

4.32 Rua do Teatro Apartments
The building is constructed from
an exposed steel frame with
carefully detailed connections.
It is staggered in massing and held
away from the party wall, inserting
itself diplomatically into the
neighbourhood. The glazed
west elevation looks toward the
ocean, and bedrooms open on
to the garden.

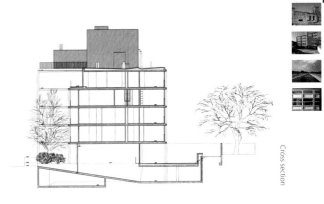

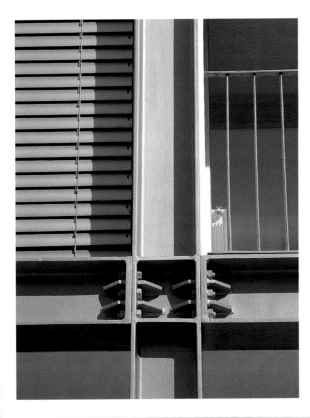

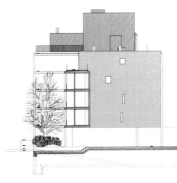

Cross section

Side elevation

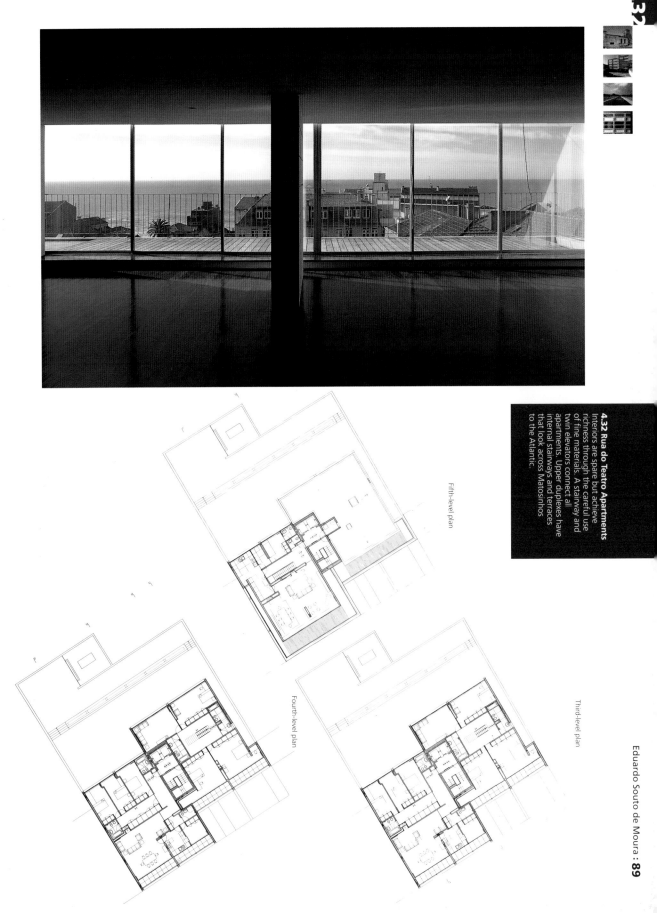

4.32 Rua do Teatro Apartments
Interiors are spare but achieve
richness through the careful use
of fine materials. A stairway and
twin elevators connect all
apartments. Upper duplexes have
internal stairways and terraces
that look across Matosinhos
to the Atlantic.

Fifth-level plan

Fourth-level plan

Third-level plan

4.33 Courtyard Housing
White walls float as abstract planes above dark timber floors and extend outside to the gardens. Minimal glazing details aid the visual penetration of each home. Interior walls, doors and furniture are designed as subsidiary planes within the overall planar composition.

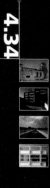

Section parallel to Avenida da Boavista

Axonometric

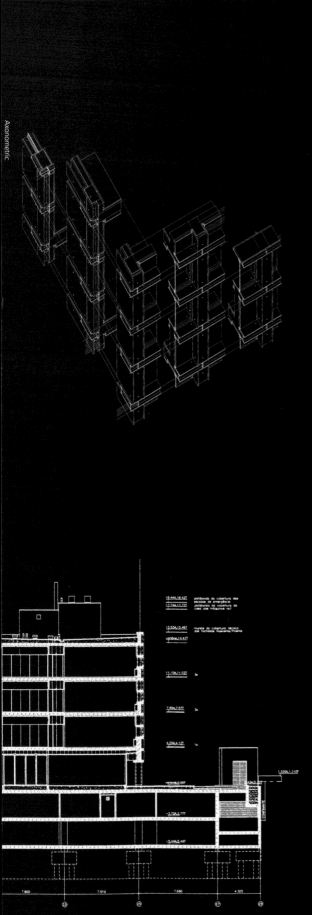

4.34 Burgo Tower

The building is designed to sit on a plinth next to its horizontal companion. The tower's skin is built up from a limited palette: deep bands of granite between slits of glass and steel on the north and south façades; and panels of glass and stone inside the exposed steel frame to the east and west. Three horizontal panels appear on every level.

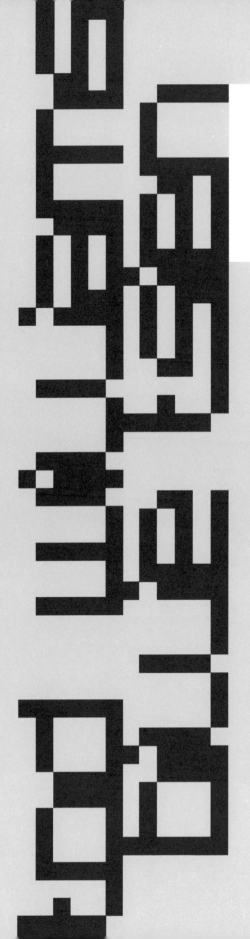

4.41

4.42

4.43

4.44

Tod Williams and Billie Tsien
Building as Research

4.40

For it is the union of the ordinary and the miraculous that makes wonder.
Thomas Wolfe[1]

The Neurosciences Institute (NSI, p. 104) is a masterpiece of contemporary American architecture. 'A monastery for scientists', according to its founder, Nobel laureate Gerald Edelman. In a splendid Californian setting, the sun-blessed NSI brings together themes of beauty and ritual, nature and construction: themes that its architects, New York–based Tod Williams and Billie Tsien, have been distilling for over two decades of collaboration. The alert slowness of their working method, their sense of research and their openness to unexpected possibilities, distinguishes their work from that of the profession, or industry, at large and from the rather fervid propositions of many theory-driven colleagues.

The studio of Tod Williams and Billie Tsien occupies a long ground-level unit on Central Park South, a few blocks from the principals' own apartment. Daily life for the architects and their dedicated young staff is thus spent in the very heart of New York City with its rich spectrum of experiences and constant bustle and tension. Attentive pedestrians passing by outside may notice various models and drawings assembled in the practice's meeting room and only screened from the pavement by domestic-size windows. The primary work of design and construction management takes place further back, in a landlocked double-height volume, so that – although projects take Williams and Tsien to California and Michigan and Arizona – the studio is inextricably part of Manhattan.

The office is somewhat reminiscent of the Sir John Soane Museum in Lincoln's Inn Fields, London. There is an intimate and characteristic calm about both places; the museum originally being Soane's town house, Williams and Tsien's office acting almost as an annexe to their own home. Whereas Soane filled his toplit rooms with such trophies of antiquity as classical paintings and statues, the New York studio is at times a messy laboratory for work in progress and a gallery of the architects' previous projects. There are drawings, models and fragments of such unrealized proposals as a raised cylinder public-housing project for Harlem, dating from the late 1980s. There are also some cubic black club chairs that were designed for New York's Asia House, the New York cultural institute, during the same period.

Originally from Detroit, Tod Williams was educated at Princeton University, then worked for six years with Richard Meier, New York's most feted architect of recent decades. As one of the city's famous Five Architects, Meier has skillfully interpreted Le Corbusier's concept of the house as 'machine to live in'. Williams also investigated these ideas, but even in his first solo building the Tarlo House on Long Island, completed in 1979, one detects a softening of Meier's purist forms, an interest less in language than in surface and place-making. Before working with Williams (Tod Williams Billie Tsien Associates was established in 1986), Billie Tsien trained first as a fine artist at Yale University, then as an architect at University of California at Los Angeles (UCLA). At least part of the firm's painterly attention to surface, its accommodation of performance or the simple pleasures of movement, is surely due to this twofold training.

To date, Williams and Tsien have had a rewardingly unorthodox career. They have directed their own open and catholic interests toward installation design (as with 'Domestic Arrangements: A Lab Report' at the Walker Art Center, Minneapolis, 1989–90) and sets for drama and dance ('The World Upside Down', Amsterdam, 1991). These temporary experiments with materiality and function, illumination and space serve to test theses or hunches that are later applied in more strictly architectural projects. The architects' appreciation of beauty, whether in artifacts from foreign cultures or in processes of industrial fabrication, recalls in part the gathering and appropriation tactics of Charles and Ray Eames in postwar Los Angeles. At the Walker, walls and small chairs were made from Homasote (a mixture of recycled newspaper and paraffin) and floors were constructed from the wood-chip pallets used to transport goods by forklift truck.

At the modest Freeman Silverman House (p. 110) in Arizona, simple elements of construction – concrete blocks, timber sheeting, punched window openings, two non-identical bridges – have been exploited to create special moments in the daily use of the home, forming an interior landscape. The clients themselves refer approvingly to Williams and Tsien's investigation of an ordinary palette as 'common materials used in an uncommon way'. The integration of everyday components, revealed and valued for their inherent physical properties, is evidence of the architects' concern not with elaborate technique per se, as in High-Tech architecture, but with normal sensory experience, an architecture of movement and perception that is most clearly manifest in the multi-part Neurosciences Institute.

Williams and Tsien used much more luxurious materials in the town house on Manhattan's East 72nd Street (1993–96), which is an extreme case of sensory design. It is a modern *Gesamtkunstwerk*, a complete spatial construct in which each surface and fixture has been considered. In the tactility and pattern of such ornamental items as the living-room carpet, one still feels the presence of nature in the design. As with the Museum of American Folk Art, also in New York (p. 118), the 72nd Street house has an urbane applied façade, a dramatic central lightwell and a manicured rear terrace. Williams and Tsien and David Chipperfield explore the possibilities of these framed or layered outdoor spaces in the urban context. The work of the Americans, however, appears more delicate, with screen devices being typically subsidiary to the primary mass or structure.

The Neurosciences Institute weaves together details and moments of construction with a positive exploitation of land surface. The buildings at La Jolla nestle into a bluff facing inland from the Pacific, subservient to the topography and each is visibly composed of many constituent pieces. The architects' intention is to allow the complex to be experienced sensuously, opening up architecture and nature to scholars and visitors alike through circulation, touch and the play of light and shade. As at the Phoenix Museum of Art (1991–94), the ground shelves, steps and ramps to facilitate experience. In Phoenix, the courtyard is still waiting for one other element: the hollow translucent pavilion proposed by Williams and Tsien as a venue for sculpture. With existing adjacent buildings beyond the designers' brief, this vessel/lantern would act as an inner beacon or communal icon for the museum.

The embankment at the NSI is made from a long line of glass-faced laboratories, cranked in plan, sloping in section and glistening in the morning light. An architectural personality is built up through such overlaying or coming together of materials and structure. Paths, ramps, indented entryways and balconies offer views into and through the entire assemblage. Rather than tailor an ideal, as Souto de Moura seems interested in doing, Williams and Tsien's rationale is inductive. The porticoed auditorium emerges with its artificial hillock as the theory building thrusts inland toward the freeway and desert hills beyond. The offices of NSI founder Gerald Edelman are in this prow, with a re-entrant terrace that is home to a split-beehive light monitor and a polished stone slab that juts into space. The small private assemblage of forms is reminiscent of Le Corbusier's more sculptural phase in the 1950s, in fact it is almost pure sculpture.

The architects' gentle exhibitionism appears again in the natatorium for Cranbrook, Williams's alma mater in Michigan. They have a special affinity for such sensuous, athletic programmes and have already built a private pool on Long Island with natural side illumination and a Sol LeWitt mural; a lap pool glowing upward from the basement of the Manhattan town house; and an 'aquatic centre' for a women's college in Upstate New York. At Cranbrook, their intention is to integrate new construction with the existing campus layout – an occasionally bucolic labyrinth – and to open up the interiors visually and physically to the woods and sky outside. Hence the carefully positioned viewing apertures, the twin oculi above the pool itself, and the vertical side louvres that mix the air of the pool with the air of the forest for the swimmers' refreshment. The roof might be considered as the latest in a family of pivoting screens and retractable membranes.

In all Williams and Tsien's work, the surface of the ground and the surface of the ceiling or the sky are crucial; walls hold these planes in place. The ground is felt by the feet as one walks about a building or area of landscape; the walls are more likely to be touched by the hand or simply brushed against. Thus the texture of wall surfaces has a vital physicality. The Museum of American Folk Art uses this sensuous aspect of walls at two scales. The intimate one, at human dimensions, as one circulates through the interior and the urban one, the great bronze broach that is discovered by the public in the hard maze of New York City. Williams and Tsien find earth-based projects natural. With the new museum building, they are consciously adding mineral substance to the city fabric, an almost shamanistic act. It promises to be a unique gesture, constructing urban art for the passer-by.

1   Wolfe, Thomas. *Look Homeward, Angel: a Story of the Buried Life* (New York: Scribner Classics, 1997)

4.4

Neurosciences Institute
La Jolla, California, 1992–95

Attached to the Scripps Institute in La Jolla, north of San Diego, the Neurosciences Institute (NSI) brings together leading researchers and theoreticians to study aspects of cognition and the workings of the human brain. Williams and Tsien developed an open collegiate plan, where principal forms work with the topography as it slopes inland from an upper access road.

Pedestrian routes wind through the plaza created by these gently fractured buildings, and cross to Scripps via an inclined walkway and a short tunnel. Practical researchers work in laboratories that are partially below ground; more abstract theoreticians share a three-storey shard to the north. Everybody congregates in the dining room and library situated in the knuckle between these two forms. A third element, an auditorium and concert hall, sits out in the plaza as a sculptural object.

Concrete, Texas fossil stone and green serpentine pavers have been sandblasted, honed and polished to achieve a painterly range of finishes. More intimate details, such as handrails, canted glass balustrades, operable redwood screens and the faceted plaster shells in the auditorium have been applied as tectonic skins to the underlying concrete support. A particular, even ornamental architecture is thus achieved through 'trial and error', by an acute sense of both construction and the interaction between building and users. Finally, the NSI nestles into its setting with judicious rows of planting, a mound of grass and a cool trough of water glinting in the sun.

Freeman Silverman House
Phoenix, Arizona, 1995–96

4.42

This 350-square-metre home for a couple with two young children is in the northern reaches of Phoenix. The entire neighbourhood is essentially desert, with little ground cover and summer temperatures reaching 50° centigrade. The immediate site is crossed by a seasonal stream, a declivity in the earth washed intermittently by flash floods and home to a rich and eclectic array of both plant and animal life. The house splits into two not-quite-parallel blocks on either side of this small ravine, connected by one external and one internal footbridge. An outdoor swimming pool, with a fountain to recycle water, and an elemental carport complete the composition.

The house is protected from the sun by outer walls of opaque concrete block, striated horizontally as if an outcrop of nature. It is marked by sharp flat parapets and a few geometric cuts. The interior, obversely, opens up through large expanses of glass to offer intimate glimpses of the stream's bed and other rooms beyond. Views are also framed north toward the Arizona mountains. The larger wing contains an entrance court, living spaces, kitchen and cave-like bedrooms for the children. The enclosed bridge, a hybrid of in-situ concrete and aluminium sheeting with low slit apertures, leads to the parents' and guest rooms in the opposite wing.

There are many subtle adjustments to the ground plane as the house navigates its site. Interior floors are terrazzo, ceilings are made from wood fibre panel, cabinetwork is maple. In the kitchen, a biomorphic concrete and granite island is the locus of family life.

Cranbrook Natatorium
Bloomfield Hills, Michigan, 1996–99

4.43

In the leafy suburb of Bloomfield Hills, Cranbrook is a remarkable community instigated by Detroit philanthropist George Booth almost a century ago, and designed primarily by the great Finnish Arts and Crafts architect Eliel Saarinen. Cranbrook comprises a renowned School of Art and Design, a Museum of Science and Junior and High Schools. The last-named is the site for Williams and Tsien's new sports facilities.

The architects' project weaves its way around existing buildings and combines old and new through form and axes and views of the campus, fusing student routine with building and landscape as envisioned by Cranbrook's founders. Williams and Tsien's sports hall and swimming pool are at a short distance from each other. The sports hall, an orthogonal box lit by splaying rooflights, reinforces one flank of the campus, toward a car park and entryway. As yet unbuilt, the sports hall will augment the already romantic skyline of Saarinen's school building.

Linking academic pursuits with the athletic, a bookstore is incorporated into the lobby of the sports hall. A courtyard pool and a picturesque pedestrian bridge lead toward the natatorium and continue Cranbrook's integration of nature and sculptural form. Completed in 1999, the 25-yard competitive pool is sited in a grove of evergreen trees, and, from inside, the red conifer trunks are horizontally framed by long low windows. Twenty-two-foot-tall (6.7 metres) mahogany louvres pivot open vertically to provide fresh air while, in summer, two conical oculi with sliding covers admit direct sunlight and occasional glimpses of sky.

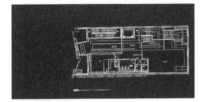

Museum of American Folk Art

Victoria, British Columbia, 1992–96

4.44

Sensations akin to those experienced in nature will be the most memorable aspect of the eight-storey structure being built for the Museum of American Folk Art on Manhattan's 53rd Street. Visitors will ascend to the fifth floor in a roomlike elevator cab, then descend slowly by various stairways, pass through exhibition spaces that that are like small plateaux or mountain terraces, and look across voids or into light wells as if in an animated valley. There is a call to human engagement and an unexpectedness about this architecture not unlike the visceral and unorthodox works it is being built to display.

The site is a thin lot facing south and surrounded by the Museum of Modern Art. Williams and Tsien propose to screen the façade with an opaque mask made of half-inch-thick white bronze panels, an extraordinary addition that will allow the comparatively small building to enter an unusual formal dialogue with its neighbours. This screen is folded to catch sunlight throughout the day and to give views out through 'cracks' to either side and around the more articulated entryway. Gallery space is above grade and a library, an auditorium, washrooms and offices in two layers of basement will be partially lit by natural light admitted through several small fissures. A bookshop at ground level and a café on a mezzanine above are planned to intensify the pedestrian experience of the city.

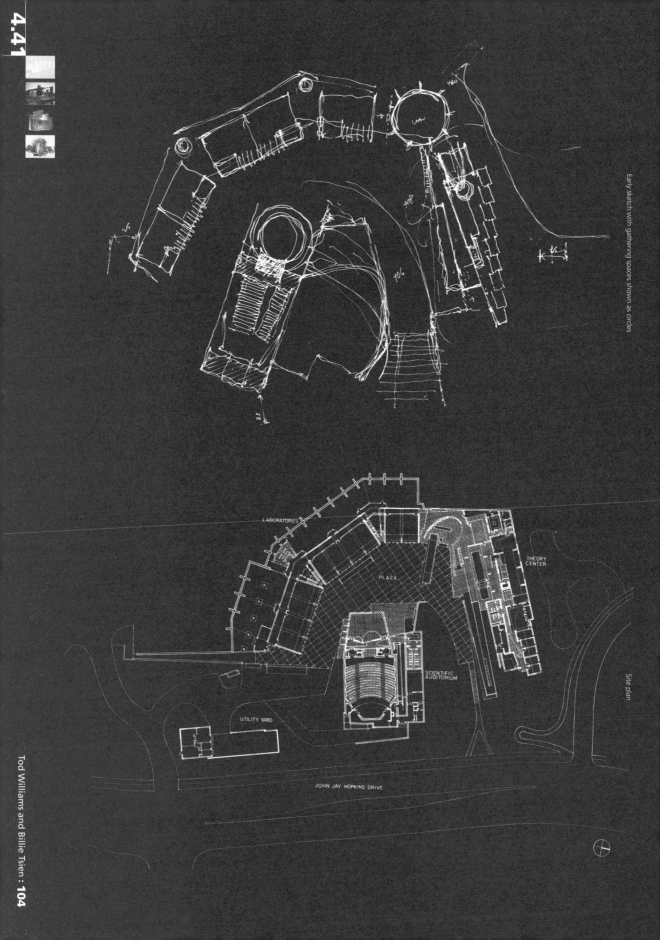

Early sketch with gathering spaces shown as circles

LABORATORIES

THEORY CENTER

PLAZA

SCIENTIFIC AUDITORIUM

UTILITY YARD

JOHN JAY HOPKINS DRIVE

Site plan

4.41 Neurosciences Institute
The plan ensures that laboratories and the theory centre embrace a communal plaza and auditorium. Gathering spaces – sketched first as circles – occur between the laboratories and theory centre and at the auditorium's entrance. Changes in material and planting help to humanize the institution.

4.41 Neurosciences Institute
The elongated pool cools the plaza, and the auditorium (right) is protected by an artificial grassy mound. Stairs lead from the plaza to the laboratories.

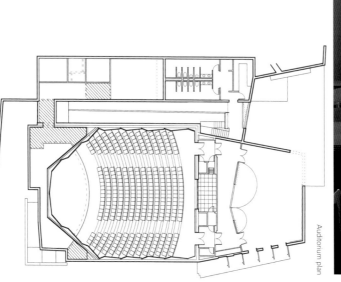

Auditorium plan

4.41 Neurosciences Institute
Practical requirements are
characteristically addressed by
legible, tactile insertions. The
auditorium has an internal plaster
skin, adjusted for musical recitals
and folded to accommodate
technical services. The roof above
the entry to the auditorium splits,
allowing a wash of natural light to
penetrate the space.

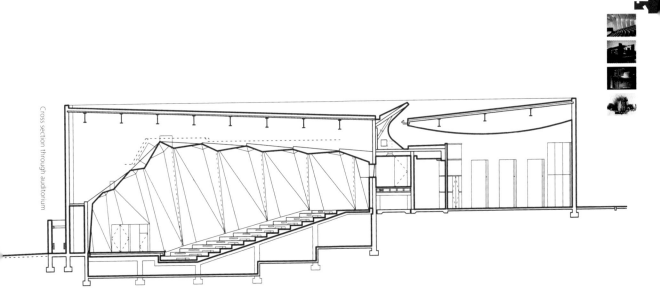

Cross section through auditorium

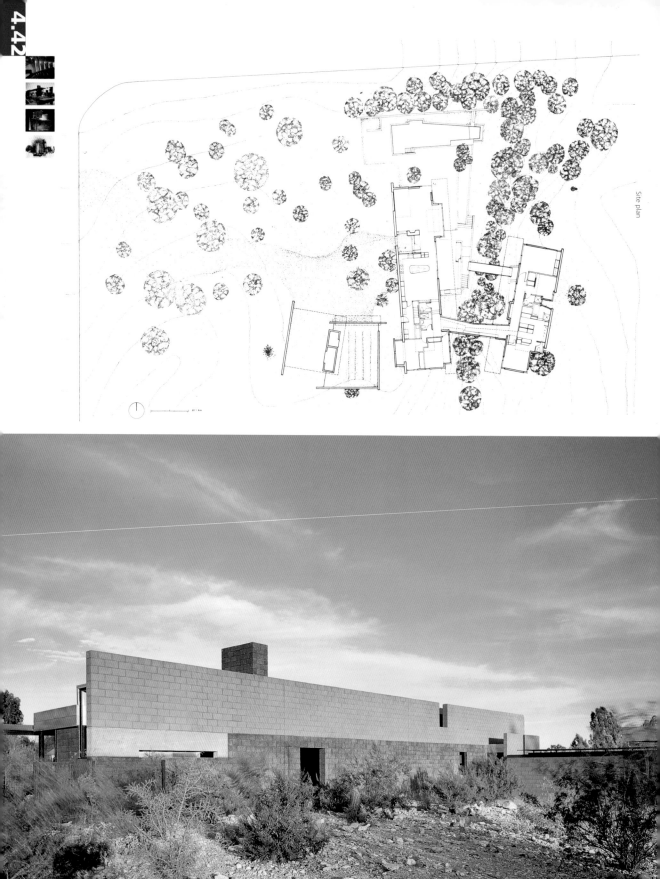

Site plan

4.42 Freeman Silverman House
Consisting of two orthogonal bars, the house is splayed about the route of a seasonal stream and connected by internal and external bridges. Entered from the cubic porch or by the door next to the carport, the house is protected from the hot desert sun by solid exterior walls to the east and west.

4.42 Freeman Silverman House
The living room clusters around the fireplace and looks out to a landscape with a small swimming pool. Interior walls of glass and the corridor in the bedroom wing face each other across the vegetation on the stream's bed. The water supply is recycled through the pool.

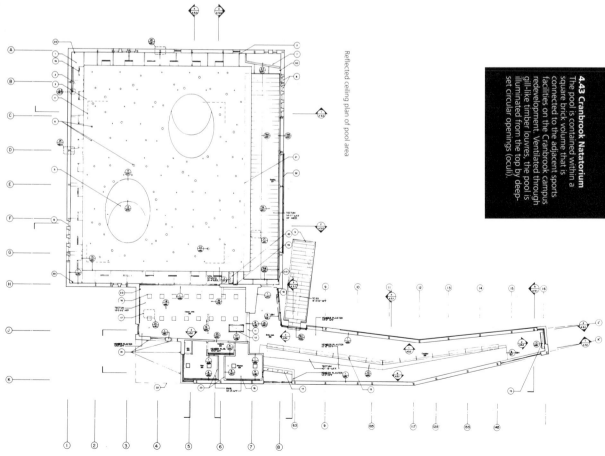

Reflected ceiling plan of pool area

4.43 Cranbrook Natatorium
The pool is contained within a
square brick volume that is
connected to the adjacent sports
facilities on the Cranbrook campus
redevelopment. Ventilated through
gill-like timber louvres, the pool is
illuminated from the top by deep-
set circular openings (oculi).

4.43 Cranbrook Natatorium
Set amid trees and around a new forecourt, the pool has low horizontal windows. Panels slide above the oculi to expose sky and natural light. The pool's ceiling also has artificial light fittings in random clusters.

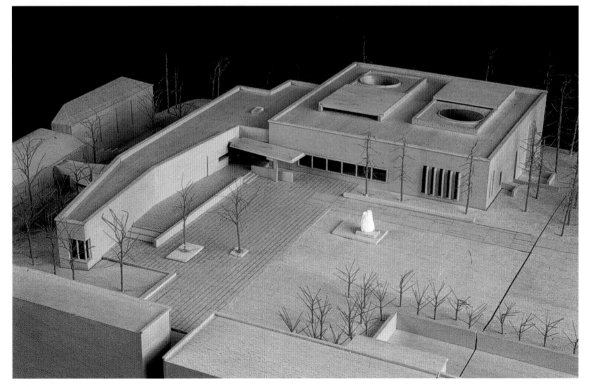

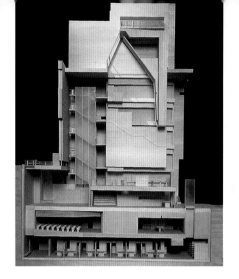

4.44 Museum of American Folk Art

The sectional model and drawing show the vertical gallery circulation route about a central lightwell. Buried or encased in midtown Manhattan, secondary voids admit light down to offices and the auditorium in the basement levels. A café is situated on a mezzanine above the entry area.

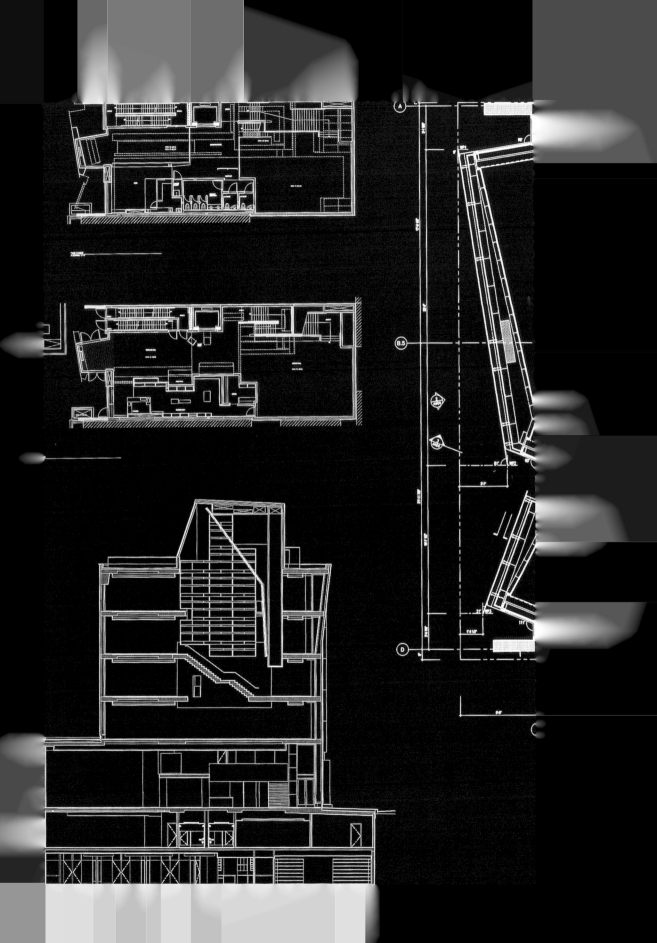

4.44 Museum of American Folk Art
Light, views and entry access are all found to the sides and from below at pavement level. The façade is a splayed surface of white bronze (here in trial pours). The building is situated close to the Museum of Modern Art.

David Chipperfield

Biographical notes

Graduating from the Architectural Association, London in 1977, David Chipperfield (born 1953) went on to work for Douglas Stephen, Richard Rogers and Norman Foster. He founded his own practice in 1984, and now has offices in London, Berlin and New York, with projects underway in Germany, Italy, Liechtenstein, Spain, the US and the UK. Chipperfield has taught at Harvard's Graduate School of Design, London's Royal College of Art, the University of Graz and the École Polytechnique in Lausanne. He has been a professor at Stuttgart's Staatliche Akademie der Bildenden Künste since 1995. Chipperfield was awarded the Heinrich Tessenow Medal in 1999, and he represented the UK at the Venice Biennale in 2000.

Select bibliography

Monographs

'David Chipperfield 1991–1997'. *El Croquis* (no. 87, includes 'A Conversation with David Chipperfield' transcribed by Adam Caruso and Peter St. John, 1998).

'David Chipperfield: Recent work'. *2G* (Barcelona: Editorial Gustavo Gili, no. 1, 1997).

Hara, Hiroshi and others. *The Japan Architect* (no. 11(3), Autumn 1993).

David Chipperfield. (Barcelona: Editorial Gustavo Gili, 1992).

Sudjic, Deyan. *Equipment Stores. Architect: David Chipperfield* (London: Wordsearch, 1992).

Articles/Features

City Visionaries: Alsop & Störmer, David Chipperfield Architects, Nigel Coates & Doug Branson, Zaha Hadid (London: The British Council, 2000).

De Michelis, Marco. 'Competition for the Extension of the San Michele Cemetery in Isola, Venice'. *Domus* (no. 817, July/August 1999).

Iloniemi, Laura. 'Kuusi Arkkitehtia Lontoosta/Six London Architects'. *Arkkitehti* (vol. 95, no. 2, 1998).

Kieren, Martin. 'Casa unifamiliare, Germania'. *Domus* (no. 795, July/August 1997).

Foster, Wayne. 'Tradition and Innovation: Timber as Rainscreen Cladding'. *ARQ: Architectural Research Quarterly* (vol. 2, no. 8, Summer 1997).

Chipperfield, David. 'Against The Rhetoric Of The New'. *Casabella* (vol. 60, no. 638, October 1996).

Field, Marcus. 'Henley's Trojan Horse'. *Blueprint* (no. 131, September 1996).

Chipperfield, David. 'River and Rowing Museum'. *UME* (no. 1, 1996).

Bernau, Nikolaus. 'Respektabel'. *Bauwelt* (vol. 85, no. 22, June 1994).

'Chipperfield in Kyoto'. *Blueprint* (no. 82, November 1991).

'Il museo privato Gotoh a Tokio'. *Casabella* (vol. 53, no. 559, July/August 1989).

Project information

River and Rowing Museum 1989–96

Team	Renato Benedetti, David Chipperfield, Jan Coghlan, Jamie Fobert, Naoko Kawamura, Haruo Morishima, Rik Nys, Jonathan Sergison
Project manager	Davis Langdon Management

Structural engineer	Whitby & Bird
Services engineer	Furness Green Partners
Quantity surveyor	Davis Langdon & Everest
Photography	Richard Bryant: pp. 25 [top], 28 [top], 33 [bottom]; David Chipperfield Architects: p. 35 [bottom]; Dennis Gilbert: pp. 18, 28 [bottom], 36; Ben Johnson: pp.28 [second from top], 33 [top], 34; Margherita Spiluttini: pp. 2, 28 [second from bottom], 35 [top], 37

House in Germany 1994–96

Team	Philipp Auer, Brigite Becker, Stevan Brown, David Chipperfield, Jamie Fobert, Mark Randel, Eva Schad, Mia Schlegel, Mechthild Stuhlmacher, Henning Stummel
Contact architect	M. J. Zielinski Dipl. Ing. Freischaffender Architect AIV/BDB
Structural engineer	Dipl. Ing. René Becker, Dipl. Ing. Gotthard Gonsior
Services engineer	Dipl. Ing. H. J. Fitz
Landscape architect	Katrin Lesser
Photography	Stefan Müller

Neues Museum 1996

Phase I

Team	Renato Benedetti, David Chipperfield, Jan Coghlan, Eamon Cushnahan, Jamie Fobert, Madeleine Lambert, Genevieve Lilley, Jonathan Sergison, Steven Shorter, Zoka Skorup, Simon Timms
Historic building consultant	Julian Harrap Architects
Structural and services engineer	Ove Arup & Partners, London (Tom Barker, Matthew Lovell, Jane Wernick)
Quantity surveyor	Tim Gatehouse Associates/Tim Gatehouse

Phases II & III

Team	Philipp Auer, Franz Borho, Nathalie Bredella, David Chipperfield, An Fonteyne, Robin Foster, Christine Hohage, Mario Hohmann, Martin Kley, Harvey Langston-Jones, Claudia Marx, Patrick McInerney, Ian McKnight, Guy Morgan-Harris, Stefan Müller, Rik Nys, Nina Nysten, Mark Randel, Donna Riley, Eva Schad, Alexander Schwarz, Haewon Shin, Graham Smith, Henning Stummel, Giuseppe Zampieri, Mark Zogrotzki
Historic building consultant	Julian Harrap Architects
Structural engineer	Ove Arup & Partners, London (Juan Alago, visitor movement study; Colin Stuart, project manager; Jane Wernick, structural consultant)
Services engineer	Ove Arup & Partners, London/Berlin (David Lewis, structural consultant; Michael Schmidt, mechanical consultant; Andrew Sedgwick, mechanical and electrical consultant)
Quantity surveyor	Tim Gatehouse Associates/Tim Gatehouse
Photography	Jörg von Bruchhausen: p. 44 [bottom]; David Chipperfield Architects: pp. 42–43 [bottom], 43; Roman März: pp. 30 [bottom], 42 [middle], 44 [top right]; Stefan Müller: pp. 25 [second from bottom], 30 [top and second from bottom], 44 [top left]

Extension to San Michele Cemetery 1998

Phase I

Team	Erik Ajemian, Ada Yvars Bravo, David Chipperfield, Daniel Lopez-Perez, Alessandra Maiolino, Giuseppe Zampieri
Structural engineer	Jane Wernick Associates
Quantity surveyor	Tim Gatehouse Associates/Tim Gatehouse
Photography	David Chipperfield Architects

Waro Kishi

4.20 Biographical notes

In 1950, Waro Kishi was born in Yokohama, Japan. At Kyoto University, he graduated from the department of electronics in 1973, from the department of architecture two years later and received a Ph.D. in architecture in 1978. He has worked at Masayuki Kurokawa Architect & Associates, and in 1981 he established his own practice in Kyoto, reorganizing it as Waro Kishi + K Architects/ Associates in 1993. Professor at Kyoto Institute of Technology (KIT), Kishi has won many awards from Japanese institutes. He represented Japan at the 1996 Venice Biennale and his work was the subject of a major exhibition at Tokyo's Gallery MA in August/ September 2000.

Select bibliography

Monographs

Watanabe, Hiroshi. *Waro Kishi* (London/Stuttgart: Edition Axel Menges, 2001).

Kishi, Waro. *PROJECTed Realities* (Tokyo: Toto Shuppan, 2000).

Bradaschia, Maurizio. *Waro Kishi – Store Design: 5 Bus Stops + 1* (Modena: Logos Art, 1999).

'Waro Kishi 1987–1996'. *El Croquis* (no. 77, 11, 1996).

Waro Kishi. Introduction by Terence Riley (Barcelona: Editorial Gustavo Gili, 1995).

Ishida, Junichiro. *Waro Kishi: Architectural Works 1987–1991* (Kyoto: Tairyu-do, 1992).

Articles/Features

Futagawa, Yukio. 'Interview'. *GA Japan* (no. 37, March 1999).

'House in Higashi-Osaka'. *The Japan Architect* (no. 28, Winter 1998).

'Memorial Hall in Yamaguchi'. *Casabella* (no. 657, June 1998).

Kishi, Waro. 'Toward a 20th-Century Vernacular'. *The Japan Architect* (no. 29, April 1998).

'Murasakino Wakuden Restaurant'. *Detail* (vol. 37, no. 8, December 1997).

'Memorial Hall in Yamaguchi'. *The Japan Architect* (no. 27, Autumn 1997).

'House in Higashi-Osaka, House in Higashinada – Disappeared City/Stopped House'. *Shinkenchiku/Jutakutokushu* (no. 135, July 1997).

Maruyama, Hiroshi. 'House in Nipponbashi, House in Shimagamo, Interview'. *Space Design* (no. 390, March 1997).

Maki, Fumihiko, Waro Kishi and Shuichi Matsumura. 'Architecture Now', *Shinkenchiku/Jutakutokushu* (no. 129, January 1997).

Kishi, Waro. 'On Architecture in Detail'. *The Japan Architect* (no. 23, September 1996).

Kishi, Waro. 'Homage to the "White House"'. *Space Design* (no. 382, July 1996).

'Murasakino Wakuden Restaurant'. *GA Japan* (no. 19, January 1996).

Yamamoto, Riken, Waro Kishi, Kazuyo Sejima and Yukio Futagawa. 'The State of the Contemporary House in Japan'. Transcription of a discussion. *GA Houses* (no. 47, 1995).

Chipperfield, David. 'Making Space: House in Nipponbashi, House in Nakagyo, Sonobe SD Office, Kim House, Auto Lab, Kyoto-Kagaku Research Institute, Yunokabashi Bridge'. *Casabella* (vol. 613, June 1994).

Ashihara, Taro, Hidetoshi Ono and Waro Kishi. 'Architect Way of the 21st Century'. *Shinkenchiku* (vol. 69, January 1994).

Kishi, Waro. 'From Central Court to Rooftop Garden'. *Quaderns* (no. 202, September 1993).

Kishi, Waro. 'About Modernism in Architecture – House in Nipponbashi, Sonobe SD Office, Weekend House in Tateshina'. *The Japan Architect* (no. 6, May 1992).

Kishi, Waro. 'Space Analyses of Maekawa's Kinokuniya Bookstore Building'. *Space Design* (no. 331, April 1992).

Furuyama, Masao. 'Far Away Emotion'. *Space Design* (no. 322, July 1991).

Project information

Murasakino Wakuden Restaurant 1994–95

Site area	55: 17 m²
Building area	35.87 m²
Total floor area	103.98 m²
Photography	Hiroyuki Hirai

Memorial Hall, Yamaguchi University 1994–97

Site area	92 631.18 m²
Building area	329.53 m²
Total floor area	626.77 m²
Photography	Hiroyuki Hirai

House in Higashi-Osaka 1995–97

Site area	115.71 m²
Building area	69.32 m²
Total floor area	186.68 m²
Photography	Hiroyuki Hirai

Roswell Hotel 1997

Site area	7200 m²
Building area	6320 m²
Total floor area	18 840 m²
Photography	Hiroyuki Hirai

Eduardo Souto de Moura

Biographical notes

Born in northern Portugal in 1952, Eduardo Souto de Moura
worked for Álvaro Siza from 1974 until 1979. In 1980,
he set up his own practice in the city of Porto, and some
of his earliest work includes such institutional projects as
the market at Braga (1980–84) and the Casa das Artes in
Porto (1988–91). Souto de Moura has taught and lectured
throughout Europe, and has participated in design
competitions in Salzburg, Venice and Berlin. He is currently
working on a winery near Valladolid in Spain.

Select bibliography

Monographs

'Eduardo Souto de Moura: Recent work'. Essays by Jacques
Lucan, Eduardo Bru and Eduardo Souto de Moura. *2G*
(no. 5, 1998/1).

Riera Ojeda, Oscar, ed. *Ten Houses: Eduardo Souto Moura*
(Gloucester, Massachusetts: Rockport Publishers, 1998).

Souto de Moura, Eduardo. *Temi di progetti/Themes for Projects*
(Milan: Skira, 1998).

Angelillo, Antonio. *Eduardo Souto Moura* (Lisbon: Blau,
1996).

Eduardo Souto de Moura. Introductions by Wilfried Wang
and Álvaro Siza (Barcelona: Editorial Gustavo Gili, 1990).

Articles/Features

Baglione, Chiara. 'Case a patio, Matosinhos, 1999'. *Casabella*
(vol. 64, no. 678, May 2000).

Di Battista, Nicola. 'Centro culturale, Oporto'. *Domus* (no. 725,
March 2000).

Gerner, Manfred. 'Umnutzung, Ergänzung, Sanierung'. *Detail*
(vol. 39, no. 7, October/November 1999).

Baglione, Chiara. 'Artificiale naturalezza, Moledo, 1998'.
Casabella (vol. 63, no. 664, February 1999).

'Rua do Teatro, Oporto'. *Cambridge Architecture Journal*,
1996/97.

Sallazzaro Arbici, Sonia and Franco Fantin. 'Edificio residentiale
a Porto'. *Domus* (no. 788, December 1996).

Honzelle, Béatrice. 'Un Parallèle en Pointillés'. *Techniques &
Architecture* (no. 425, April/May, 1996).

'Eduardo Souto de Moura – Edificio de viviendas'. *Quaderns*
(no. 212, 1996).

Dos Santos, José Paulo. 'Dipartimento di Geologia, Università
di Aveiro, Portogallo'. *Domus* (no. 773, July/August 1995).

Gazzaniga, Luca. 'Due case in Portogallo'. *Domus* (no. 768,
February 1995).

Fernandes, José Manuel. *581 Architects in the World* (Tokyo:
Toto Shuppan, 1995).

Montaner, Josep Maria. 'Minimalismos'. *El Croquis*
(no. 62–63, 1993).

Di Battista, Nicola. 'Eduardo Souto de Moura, Tre interni in
Portogallo'. *Domus* (no. 741, September, 1992).

Dijk, Hans van. 'Cultureel Centrum in Porto van Eduardo Souto
de Moura'. *Archis* (no. 6, June 1991).

Wang, Wilfried. 'Arquitectos de Oporto: Távora, Siza, Souto
Moura, Una identidad no lineal'. *Arquitectura, Revista del
COAM* (Colegio Oficial de Arquitectos de Madrid, vol. 67,
no. 261 (4), July/August 1986).

4.30

Project information

Pousada Santa Maria do Bouro 1989–97

Team	Marie Clement, Ana Fortuna, Manuela Lara, Pedro Valenta
Contractor	Soares da Costa
Structural engineer	G O P
Photography	Luís Ferreira Alves

Courtyard Housing 1993

Team	Silvia Alves, Filipe Pinto da Cruz, Teresa Gonçalves, Manuela Lara, Laura Peretti
Contractor	Composto
Structural engineer	G O P
Photography	Luís Ferreira Alves

Rua do Teatro Apartments 1992–95

Team	Graça Correia, Francisco Cunha, Manuela Lara
Contractor	Soares de Costa/San José
Structural engineer	Cdo
Photography	Luís Ferreira Alves

Burgo Tower 1991

Team	Silvia Alves, Teresa Gonçalves, Pedro Reis
Structural engineer	Adão da Fonseca & Associados
Photography	Luís Ferreira Alves

Tod Williams and Billie Tsien

Biographical notes

In 1967, Tod Williams received a master's degree in fine arts and architecture from Princeton University. He worked for Richard Meier between 1967 and 1973, and then established his own practice. Williams was awarded an advanced fellowship to the American Academy in Rome (1982), and elected Fellow of the American Institute of Architects (1992).

Billie Tsien holds a degree in fine arts from Yale University (1971) and a master's degree in architecture from University of California at Los Angeles (1977). She joined Williams's office in 1977, becoming a full partner in 1986.

Both architects have taught at such schools as Harvard, Parsons, Yale, University of Texas at Austin and the Southern California Institute of Architecture (SCI-ARC). The practice has won four National AIA (American Institute of Architects) Awards and the prestigious Chrysler Award for Innovation in Design (1998).

Select bibliography

Monographs

Williams, Tod and Billie Tsien. *Work/Life: Williams Tsien* (New York: The Monacelli Press, 2000).

'Williams Tsien: works'. Contributions from Elias Torres, Peter Zumthor and Will Bruder. *2G* (Barcelona: Editorial Gustavo Gili, no. 9, 1999/1).

Massarente, Alessandro. *Instituto di Scienze Neurologiche a La Jolla* (Florence: ALINEA, 1998).

Articles/Features

Cramer, Ned. 'Williams Natatorium'. *Architecture* (October 2000).

Betsky, Aaron. 'Beschutting tegen de storm/Shelter from the storm'. *Archis* (no. 3, March 1999).

'Museum of American Folk Art, New York, USA'. *Zodiac* (January/June 1999).

Ryan, Raymund. 'nature : fabric : beauty'. *Architecture + Urbanism* (no. 320, 97:06).

Miro, Marsha and Mark Carr. 'Il sogno di Cranbrook'. *Casabella* (vol. 61, no. 644, April 1997).

Ockman, Joan. 'Casa a Manhattan'. *Casabella* (vol. 61, no. 642, February 1997).

Sorkin, Michael. 'Phoenix Art Museum'. *Architectural Record* (vol.185, no. 1, January 1997).

Ingersoll, Richard. 'Block House'. *Architecture* (vol. 87, no. 6, June 1996).

Ryan, Raymund. 'Brainwatch'. *Blueprint* (February 1996).

Freiman, Ziva. 'The Brain Exchange'. *Progressive Architecture* (April 1995).

MacKeith, Peter. 'Tod Williams/Billie Tsien Interview'. *Arkkitehti* (vol. 91, no.5/6, 1994).

Nesbit, Kate. 'New College, University of Virginia, Charlottesville, Virginia'. *Skala* (no. 29, 1993).

Williams, Tod and Billie Tsien. 'Domestic Arrangements'. *Domus* (no. 717, June 1990).

Project information

Neurosciences Institute 1992–95

Principals	Tod Williams and Billie Tsien with Joseph Wong Design Associates
Team	David van Handel (project architect); Peter Arnold, Matthew Baird, Peter Burns, Betty Chen, Brett Ettinger, Martin Finio, Erika Hinrichs, Matthew Pickner, Vivian Wang
Structural engineer	Severud Associates
Mechanical engineer	Tsuchiyama, Kaino & Gibson
Electrical engineer	Randall Lamb Associates

Consulting engineer	Ambrosino, dePinto & Schneider
Acoustical consultant	Dr. Cyril M. Harris
Landscape architect	Burton Associates
Photography	J. Fluker: pp. 23, 100 [second from top and bottom], 105 [top], 106 [bottom], 108; Owen Mc Goldrick: pp. 14, 97 [top], 100 [top], 109 [bottom]; Michael Moran: pp. 100 [second from bottom], 105 [middle and bottom], 106 [top], 107

Freeman Silverman House 1995–96

Principals	Tod Williams and Billie Tsien
Project architect	Betty Chen
Contractor	GM Hunt Builders
Structural engineer	Mark Rudow
Mechanical engineer	Roy Otterbein
Photography	Michael Moran

Cranbrook Natatorium 1996–99

Principals	Tod Williams and Billie Tsien
Team	Martin Finio (project architect); Kyra Clarkson, Leslie Hanson, Vivian Wang
Contractor	Hechristmas Company
Structural engineer	Severud Associates
Mechanical engineer	Ambrosino, dePinto & Schmeider
Lighting consultants	Rick Shaver, Edison Price
Landscape architect	Peter Osler
Photography	Michael Moran

Museum of American Folk Art 1992–96

Principals	Tod Williams and Billie Tsien with Peter Guggenheimer
Team	Matthew Baird (project architect); Hana Kassem, Phil Ryan, Jennifer Stevenson
Structural engineer	Severud Associates
Mechanical engineer	Ambrosino, dePinto & Schmeider
Construction manager	F. J. Sciame Construction
Photography	Bernstein Associates: p. 103 [top]; Michael Moran: pp. 103 [second from top and bottom], 118, 120

Illustration credits

(pp. 1–23) **Frontmatter**: p. 1 House in Germany, David Chipperfield (Stefan Müller); p. 2 River and Rowing Museum, David Chipperfield (Margherita Spiluttini); p. 3 Murasakino Wakuden Restaurant, Waro Kishi (Hiroyuki Hirai); p. 4 House in Higashi-Osaka, Waro Kishi (Hiroyuki Hirai); p. 5 Rua do Teatro Apartments, Eduardo Souto de Moura (Luís Ferreira Alves); p. 6 Pousada Santa Maria do Bouro, Eduardo Souto de Moura (Luís Ferreira Alves); p. 7 Freeman Silverman House, Tod Williams and Billie Tsien (Michael Moran); p. 8 Cranbrook Natatorium, Tod Williams and Billie Tsien (Michael Moran); **Introduction**: p. 14 Neurosciences Institute, Tod Williams and Billie Tsien (Owen Mc Goldrick); p. 16 Pousada Santa Maria do Bouro, Eduardo Souto de Moura (Luís Ferreira Alves); p. 17 Rua do Teatro Apartments, Eduardo Souto de Moura (Luís Ferreira Alves); p. 18 River and Rowing Museum, David Chipperfield (Dennis Gilbert); p. 19 House in Germany, David Chipperfield (Stefan Müller); p. 20 Murasakino Wakuden Restaurant, Waro Kishi (Hiroyuki Hirai); p. 21 Murasakino Wakuden Restaurant, Waro Kishi (Hiroyuki Hirai); p. 22 Cranbrook Natatorium, Tod Williams and Billie Tsien (Michael Moran); p. 23 Neurosciences Institute, Tod Williams and Billie Tsien (J. Fluker)

Cover design: *background image* Cranbrook Natatorium (Tod Williams and Billie Tsien, photograph by Michael Moran); *front, from top* House in Germany (David Chipperfield, photograph by Stefan Müller), Murasakino Wakuden Restaurant (Waro Kishi, photograph by Hiroyuki Hirai), Courtyard Housing (Eduardo Souto de Moura, photograph by Luís Ferreira Alves), Cranbrook Natatorium (Tod Williams and Billie Tsien, photograph by Michael Moran); *back, from top* River and Rowing Museum (David Chipperfield, photograph by Margherita Spiluttini), Memorial Hall, Yamaguchi University (Waro Kishi, photograph by Hiroyuki Hirai), Pousada Santa Maria do Bouro (Eduardo Souto de Moura, photograph by Luís Ferreira Alves), Neurosciences Institute (Tod Williams and Billie Tsien, photograph by J. Fluker); *back flap, from top* River and Rowing Museum (David Chipperfield, photograph by Ben Johnson), House in Higashi-Osaka (Waro Kishi, photograph by Hiroyuki Hirai), Pousada Santa Maria do Bouro (Eduardo Souto de Moura, photograph by Luís Ferreira Alves), Neurosciences Institute (Tod Williams and Billie Tsien, photograph by Owen Mc Goldrick); *inside cover, front* Memorial Hall, Yamaguchi University (Waro Kishi, photograph by Hiroyuki Hirai); *inside cover, back* Neurosciences Institute (Tod Williams and Billie Tsien, photograph by Michael Moran)

Any copy of this book issued by the publisher as a paperback is sold subject to the condition that it shall not by way of trade or otherwise be lent, resold, hired out or otherwise circulated without the publisher's prior consent in any form of binding or cover other than that in which it is published and without a similar condition including these words being imposed on a subsequent purchaser.

First published in the United Kingdom in 2001 by Thames & Hudson Ltd, 181A High Holborn, London WC1V 7QX

© 2001 Thames & Hudson Ltd, London

All Rights Reserved. No part of this publication may be reproduced or transmitted in any form or by any means, electronic or mechanical, including photocopy, recording or any other information storage and retrieval system, without prior permission in writing from the publisher.

British Library Cataloguing-in-Publication Data
A catalogue record for this book is available from the British Library

ISBN 0-500-28267-6

Printed and bound in China by Everbest Printing Co. Ltd.